BOOKKEEPING

MANUAL AND COMPUTERISED

JOHN ROCHE

GILL & MACMILLAN

Gill & Macmillan Ltd
Hume Avenue
Park West
Dublin 12

with associated companies throughout the world

www.gillmacmillan.ie

© 2001 John Roche

0 7171 3240 4

CONTENTS   Page

Page

INTRODUCTION

This book is designed to cover the course for Bookkeeping – Manual and Computerised at National Council for Vocational Awards (NCVA) Level 2. Since bookkeeping is a very practical task, this book is designed to explain the process of bookkeeping using practical tasks at each step of the process from source documents to trial balance.

Part 1 provides students with the necessary knowledge and techniques in order to operate a manual bookkeeping system. This section presents 33 individual tasks together with detailed explanations on how to carry out each task and the solution to each task. The section concludes with two further exercises each of which requires the student to repeat all 33 tasks.

Part 2 deals with the Computer Principles section of the course and is written in a very practical, easy-to-understand manner.

Part 3 deals with the computerised bookkeeping method. This book uses TAS Books Accounting Plus to explain the computerised process, but the work can easily be applied to any computerised accounting program. This section has 41 tasks, which follow the same sequence as the manual section, and includes the additional topics such as report printing, backup files and restore files. Each task is clearly explained and includes the screens as they appear for each task.

This section also includes a transaction summary, which provides a quick reference on how to perform any of the tasks necessary for this course with program references and page references to the detail for each task. The section concludes with two further exercises each of which requires the student to repeat all 41 tasks.

Part 4 is not specifically part of the NCVA course. This section deals with the installation of TAS Books Accounting Plus, the creation of a company and the setting up of a company. Each step of the process is clearly explained in a step-by-step manner including the screens as they appear during the process. This section also includes a summary, consisting of 20 easy steps to installing the software, creating a company and setting up a company with program references, and page references to the detail in the book, for each step.

Part 5 provides all the necessary source documents which are required in order to carry out the individual tasks set in this book.

Part 6 provides a sample manual assignment and computerised examination for the NCVA assessment of the module Bookkeeping – Manual and Computerised. This section also includes solutions and a detailed marking scheme for each.

This book uses the Euro symbol for currency, but any other currency symbol may be substituted instead of the Euro symbol.

The year digits on all documents have been deliberately substituted with the symbols ## so that the book is not year-specific, thereby allowing for the use of the book, including the source documents for any year.

ACCOUNTING TERMS AND VALUE ADDED TAX (VAT)

Accounting Terms

Before we begin our work we must firstly understand a few basic terms:

1 Source Document: All entries made in the company books originate from a source document. A source document contains all the data relating to a sale, a purchase or any other transaction affecting the company. The relevant details from the source document are transferred to the appropriate daybook.

The most common source documents are:

Sales Invoices
Sales Credit Notes
Purchase Invoices
Purchase Credit Notes
Customer (Debtor) Receipts (cash or cheques received)
Supplier (Creditor) Payments (usually a remittance advice)
Petty Cash Vouchers
Record of any other payments made (e.g. VAT, Salaries, PAYE/PRSI)
Record of any other monies received (e.g. Dividend, VAT repayment)

2 Daybook: This is a book or more commonly a card or sheet onto which are written the individual daily transactions of a business. Daybooks will be examined in more detail later.

3 Account: This is one particular person's or item's details including all transactions for that account.

4 Ledger: This is a book containing all the accounts of a particular type.

Sales Ledger: This may also be called the Debtors' Ledger and contains Customers' accounts.

Purchase Ledger: This may also be called the Creditors' Ledger and contains Suppliers' accounts.

Nominal Ledger: This may also be called the General Ledger and is where all transaction end up via various routes. Entries are normally transferred from the other books or ledgers, but it is also possible to make entries directly into the nominal ledger.

5 Debit: This is an amount written in the Debit (Dr) column of a daybook or ledger. Some accounts are referred to as Debit accounts because the balance in the account at any particular time will normally be a Debit amount.

6 Credit: This is an amount written in the Credit (Cr) column of a daybook or ledger. Some accounts are referred to as Credit accounts because the balance in the account at any particular time will normally be a Credit amount. One of the most important things to learn is whether an entry in a ledger is a Debit or Credit entry. This will be explained when we are dealing with ledger entries.

VAT

This is a tax which is charged on goods and services. This tax is imposed by the Government and businesses are required by law to collect this tax and forward it to the Collector General every two months. When a business sells a good or service they add on the appropriate amount of VAT to the cost of the goods.

In the operation of any accounts, there are a number of different VAT rates which will be used. It is essential that you understand the different VAT rates. In the case of computerised accounting the program keeps track of each VAT rate by using a separate VAT code for each separate rate and produces a report listing all VAT rates for the purpose of making VAT returns to the Revenue Commissioner.

In the manual system the Net amount of the goods are recorded at the various VAT rates and in this way it is possible to calculate the VAT at the various rates.

There are eight different VAT rates in common use at present. The computer uses a code to reference each of these VAT rates. These VAT rates are determined by Government and may change from time to time. The VAT rates and the computer codes used are as follows:

Code	Rate	Description
1	20% Resale	This standard rate applies to goods which are sold or which are purchased for the purpose of selling again and which have a rate of 20% applied to them.
2	12.5% Resale	This is the same as the first rate but applies to items (usually services) which have a rate of 12.5% applied to them.
3	0% Resale	This rate is the same as the above but applies to items which have a 0% VAT rate applied to them.
4	Exempt Resale	This only applies to companies which have a section 13A VAT exemption certificate. This certificate can be obtained by companies who export more than 75% of their produce.
5	20% Non-resale	This rate applies to all goods, having a rate of 20%, which are purchased for use by the company in running their business and which will not be resold.
6	12.5% Non-resale	This is the same as the above but applies to items which have a rate of 12.5% applied to them.
7	0% Non-resale	This is the same as the above but applies to items which have a rate of 0% VAT rate applied to them.
8	Exempt Non-resale	This rate also only applies to companies which have a Section 13A exemption certificate.
9	Outside Scope Rate	Outside the VAT scope. We will not be using this but it must be set up as it is a default rate.
M	Multiple Rates	The computer program also understands the character M as a VAT Code and this is used where more than one VAT rate is used when entering a source document and therefore more than one code is required.

PART I

MANUAL
BOOKKEEPING

1. Manual Bookkeeping

In order to run any business efficiently it is essential to keep proper accounts. A good system for manually keeping accounts has been devised over the years and is well tried and tested. This system is known as the Double Entry system and we will be using this system to record the normal transactions in a business on a day-to-day basis. These day-to-day records will then be posted to the necessary ledgers in order to keep the company accounts up to date and to produce a trial balance.

We will also be using a computerised accounts system to perform the same work and you will be able to compare both systems.

The manual accounts system uses the following daybooks and ledgers:

- Daybooks
  Sales/Sales Returns Daybooks
  Purchases/Purchases Returns Daybooks
  Cash Receipts (Bank Lodgement) Book
  Cash (Bank) Payments Book
  Petty Cash Book
  General Journal

- Ledgers
  Sales (Debtors) Ledger
  Purchases (Creditors) Ledger
  Nominal (General) Ledger

We will examine the operation of each of these individually using examples in each case. A summary diagram of the bookkeeping process is shown on the next page.

It is sometimes difficult to know where to start teaching bookkeeping. Some would suggest that the obvious place to start is with purchasing as you cannot have a business without first buying something. This is a valid point but I find it very difficult to start at this point as we know nothing about the business.

I have found that the most successful point to start is with sales. If someone started work in an office of a business, it is most likely that they would be dealing with sales long before they would be dealing with purchases. This allows us to become familiar with the type of business, stock items, prices, etc. and gradually get to know the running of the business in a logical manner.

Bookkeeping – Summary Diagram

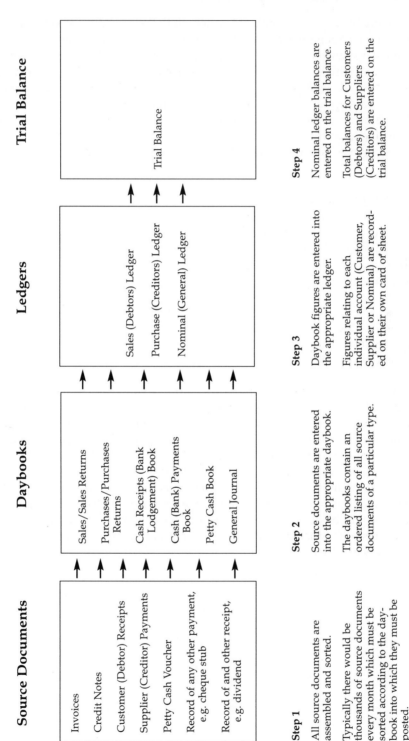

Source Documents

Invoices

Credit Notes

Customer (Debtor) Receipts

Supplier (Creditor) Payments

Petty Cash Voucher

Record of any other payment, e.g. cheque stub

Record of and other receipt, e.g. dividend

Step 1

All source documents are assembled and sorted.

Typically there would be thousands of source documents every month which must be sorted according to the day-book into which they must be posted.

Daybooks

Sales/Sales Returns

Purchases/Purchases Returns

Cash Receipts (Bank Lodgement) Book

Cash (Bank) Payments Book

Petty Cash Book

General Journal

Step 2

Source documents are entered into the appropriate daybook.

The daybooks contain an ordered listing of all source documents of a particular type.

Ledgers

Sales (Debtors) Ledger

Purchase (Creditors) Ledger

Nominal (General) Ledger

Step 3

Daybook figures are entered into the appropriate ledger.

Figures relating to each individual account (Customer, Supplier or Nominal) are record-ed on their own card or sheet.

Trial Balance

Trial Balance

Step 4

Nominal ledger balances are entered on the trial balance.

Total balances for Customers (Debtors) and Suppliers (Creditors) are entered on the trial balance.

Source Documents

All entries made in the company books originate with a source document. The relevant details from the source document are entered into the appropriate daybook. It is worth noting at this stage that the work of the bookkeeper is to record accurately the data from the source document and not to change the document if s/he thinks there is an error on it.

The source documents which we will be using are:
- – Sales Invoices
- – Sales Credit Notes
- – Purchase Invoices
- – Purchase Credit Notes
- – Customer (Debtor) Receipts (cash or cheques received)
- – Supplier (Creditor) Payments (usually a remittance advice or a cheque counterfoil)
- – Petty Cash Vouchers
- – Record of any other payments made (e.g. VAT, Salaries, PAYE/PRSI)

It is essential to become familiar with source documents and be able to identify the necessary data which needs to be recorded in the relevant daybook. The following is a typical invoice with the relevant data identified. However, invoices differ in shape, size and layout and students should become familiar with as many as possible.

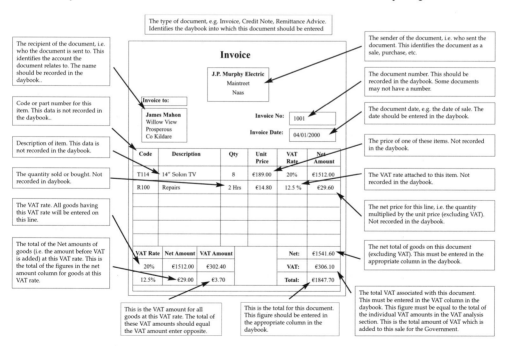

2. Daybooks

A company will have a number of books into which the data from the source documents will be entered. These books are referred to as *daybooks, books of first entry* or *books of prime entry*.

The daybooks are:

- Sales/Sales Returns Daybook
- Purchases/Purchases Returns Daybook
- Cash Receipts (Bank Lodgement) Book
- Cash (Bank) Payments Book
- Petty Cash Book
- General Journal

The use of each of these books will be explained individually, in this section.

Sales/Sales Returns Daybook

The first book which we will be using is the sales/sales returns daybook. In our case we will use a single book (page) for the sales and the sales returns. Some businesses may use separate books (pages) for the sales and the sales returns, but both systems are in common use.

The source documents for writing up this book are the invoices and credit notes issued by our company, i.e. the company you are working for. Entries in the daybook should be in date order.

We will now commence work with our first task. In order to perform this task you should have a Sales/Sales Return Daybook (sheet – Source Documents page 102).

> **Task M-1**
>
> Enter the Sales Invoice on Source Documents page 2 into the Sales/Sales Returns Daybook

This task requires you to enter the details from the invoice into the Sales/Sales Returns Daybook.

Every time an invoice or credit note is issued to a customer the data from the document is entered into the Sales/Sales Returns Daybook. This Daybook has a number of columns into which entries should be made, as follows:

Date:	The date of the invoice or credit note should be entered in this column. Entries should be in date order.
Customer:	The customer name should be entered in this column.
F:	The F stands for folio which is used to trace this entry in the company books. The folio here will usually be the initials of the sales ledger (SL) as that is where this posting will appear. The folio is usually inserted when the entry is being posted to the ledger and may also contain a number which references that particular account in the sales ledger. Posting to ledgers will be explained later.
Inv./Cr. Note Number:	This column contains the invoice or credit note number as displayed on the invoice or credit note.
Total:	The gross total amount on the invoice/credit note including VAT should be recorded in this column.
Net Amounts:	There may be two, three or more columns used to record the net amount of goods at various VAT rates. These amounts are normally totalled on the invoice, but if not then it is a simple matter of totalling the net amounts at the various VAT rates from each line of the invoice.
VAT Amount:	This column records the total VAT amount as shown on the invoice or credit note.
Sales Analysis:	The sales analysis columns are used to group the sales of various items into categories which the management of the company require to be categorised as one group. The net amount of the goods recorded on the invoice or credit note are then divided into a number of different categories and entered in the appropriate analysis column.

In this example the items are analysed into two groups, namely sales and repairs. However there may be any number of analysis columns. The totals of these columns record the amount of income for that particular group and would be recorded in a separate account in the Nominal (General) Ledger as will be explained later.

When you have completed this task your daybook should look like the following:

Company Name: J.P. Murphy Electric

Sales/Sales Returns Daybook   **Month:** January ##

Date	Customer	F	Inv./Cr. Note Number	Total	Net Amount @ 20%	@ 12.5%	VAT Amount	← Analysis → Sales	Repairs
06/01/##	James Mahon		1001	€453.60	€378.00	—	€75.60	€378.00	—

Task M-2

Enter the Sales Invoice on Source Documents pages 3–6 into the Sales/Sales Returns Daybook

Task M-3

Enter the Sales Credit Note on Source Documents page 7 into the Sales/Sales Returns Daybook

The entry of the credit note is the same as the entry of the invoice with the exception that all the money amounts must be recorded as minus amounts. This is done by placing the amount in brackets or by placing a minus sign in front of each amount. In recording figures it is very easy to fail to notice a minus in front of a number and therefore it is common practice in accounting to place the amount in brackets to indicate a minus amount. It is also a good idea to use a different colour for the recording of credit notes, however, it should be clearly understood that the colour of the entry has no significance.

 NOTE: *1. In the case of Credit Notes the amounts are recorded as minus values by placing a minus sign in front of the figure or by placing the figure in brackets.*

2. The entries in the Sales/Sales Returns Daybook must be subsequently posted to the correct ledger account. The posting of these entries will be explained later.

Completed Sales/Sales Returns Daybook for January after entering transactions

Company Name: J.P. Murphy Electric

Sales/Sales Returns Daybook   **Month:** January ##

Date	Customer	F	Inv./Cr. Note Number	Total	Net Amount @ 20%	@ 12.5%	VAT Amount	← Analysis → Sales	Repairs
06/01/##	James Mahon		1001	€453.60	€378.00	—	€75.60	€378.00	—
07/01/##	The Electrical Shop		1002	€1847.70	€1512.00	€29.60	€306.10	€1512.00	€29.60
09/01/##	New Age Contractors		1003	€4952.85	€4058.00	€74.00	€820.85	€4058.00	€74.00
11/01/##	Cash Sale		1004	€49.95	—	€44.40	€5.55	—	€44.40
12/01/##	Tomorrows Electronics		1005	€4279.50	€3483.00	€88.80	€707.70	€3483.00	€88.80
13/01/##	New Age Contractors		1006	(€549.60)	(€458.00)	—	(€91.60)	(€458.00)	—

NOTE: *The folio (F) reference (SL in this case) is usually not entered until the figures are transferred to the ledger.*

Summary Note

Sales Invoices and Credit Notes are entered in the Sales/Sales Returns Daybook

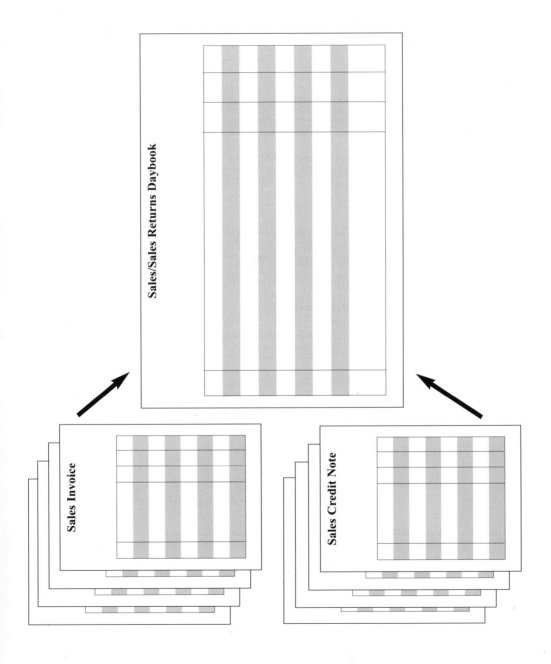

Cash Receipts (Bank Lodgement) Book

In the running of any business all monies received must be accurately recorded. All monies received, whether cheques or cash, will be lodged to a bank account. These receipts are recorded in the Cash Receipts (Bank Lodgement) Book.

The Cash Receipts (Bank Lodgement) Book is the second daybook which we will be using. All receipts should be recorded separately, with each individual receipt occupying a single line in the Cash Receipts (Bank Lodgement) Book. Since lodgements to the bank are normally only done once per day, all the receipts for that day will have the same lodgement number.

Another method used to record receipts is an analysed cash book but this method will not be explained in this book.

We will now continue our work with the next task. You will require a Cash Receipts (Bank Lodgement) Book (sheet – Source Documents page 103) in order to perform this task.

Task M-4

The first cheque on Source Documents page 8 was received from James Mahon and was lodged in the bank on the date of receipt. Enter this lodgement in the Cash Receipts (Bank Lodgement) Book.

This task requires you to enter the details from the cheque into the Cash Receipts (Bank Lodgement) Book. The source document in this case is the cheque from the customer.

The entries in the Cash Receipts (Bank Lodgement) Book are as follows:

Date:	The date of the lodgement should be entered in this column. In the case of cheques received it is the date of the lodgement which should be entered and not the date on the cheque. In the case of cash sales it is the date of the sale, as the money is received immediately.
Details:	The details of this lodgement, such as the customers name or cash sale.
Lodge No.:	The lodgement number for this lodgement. (Remember where there are a number of items lodged at the same time they will all have the same lodgement number.)
F:	This stands for folio and is the ledger reference for tracing this posting in the company books. The folio will usually be SL (sales ledger) as nearly all monies received will be from customers. The folio is usually inserted when the entry is being posted to the ledger and may also contain a number which references that particular account in the sales ledger. Posting to ledgers will be explained later.
Bank:	The amount lodged to the bank for this entry. This will be the amount of the cheque or cash.

Cash Sales: If the money is for a cash sale then the amount is entered under the Cash Sales column

Debtors: If the money is from a customer (debtor) then the amount is entered under the Debtors column.

Other: The amount of this lodgement which is not for cash sales or from a debtor is entered in this column. Any entry in this column will have a note in the side margin explaining what the lodgement is for.

Company Name: J.P. Murphy Electric

Cash Receipts (Bank Lodgement) Book   **Month:** January ##

Date	Details	Lodge No.	F	Bank	Cash Sales	Debtors	Other
10/01/##	James Mahon cheque 204587	101		€453.60	—	€453.60	—

Task M-5

Enter the Cash Sale on Source Documents page 5 into the Cash Receipts (Bank Lodgement) Book. The lodgement number is 102.

The date used for the entry of the cash sale is the date on the invoice as the money is lodged to the bank on the date of sale. In some businesses, where the amount of cash sales would be very small there may not be a lodgement every day and in such cases the lodgement date may be different from the invoice date. Another method of dealing with cash sales is to use a cash till and to lodge the till takings to the bank in a single entry.

Task M-6

Enter the cheques received on Source Documents pages 8–9 into the Cash Receipts (Bank Lodgement) Book.

NOTE: *The entries in the Cash Receipts (Bank Lodgement) Book must be subsequently posted to the correct ledger account. The posting of these entries will be explained later.*

Completed Cash Receipts (Bank Lodgement) Book for January after entering transations

Company Name: J.P. Murphy Electric

Cash Receipts (Bank Lodgement) Book   **Month:** January ##

Date	Details	Lodge No.	F	Bank	Cash Sales	Debtors	Other
10/01/##	James Mahon (cheque 204587)	101		€453.60	—	€453.60	—
11/01/##	Cash Sale	102		€49.95	€49.95	—	—
21/01/##	The Electrical Shop (cheque 215687)	103		€1847.70	—	€1847.70	—
22/01/##	New Age Contractors (cheque 272357)	104		€4403.25	—	€4403.25	—
25/01/##	Tomorrows Electronics (cheque 467832)	105		€4000.00	—	€4000.00	—

NOTE: *The folio (F) reference (SL in this case) is usually not entered until the figures are transferred to the ledger.*

Summary Note

Cheques and cash received are entered into the Cash Receipts (Bank Lodgement) Book.

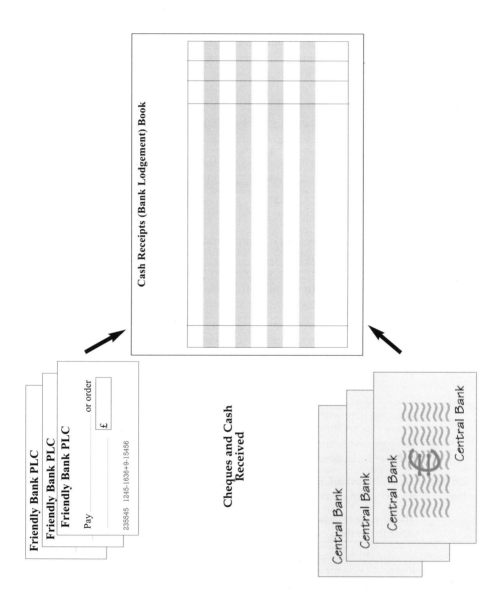

Purchases/Purchases Returns Daybook

The next book which we will be using is the Purchases/Purchases Returns Daybook. In our case we will use a single book (page) for the purchases and the purchases returns. As in the case of sales some businesses may use separate books (pages) for the purchases and the purchases returns, but again both systems are in common use.

The source documents for writing up this book are the invoices and credit notes received by our company from suppliers. Entries in the daybook should be in date order.

We will now perform the next task. In order to perform this task you should have a Purchases/Purchases Return Daybook (sheet – Source Documents page 104).

> **Task M-7**
>
> Enter the Purchase Invoice on Source Documents page 10 into the Purchases/Purchases Returns Daybook.

This task requires you to enter the details from the invoice into the Purchases/Purchases Returns Daybook.

Every time an invoice or credit note is received from a supplier the data from the document is entered into the Purchases/Purchases Returns Daybook. This Daybook has a number of columns into which entries should be made, as follows:

Date:	The date of the invoice or credit note should be entered in this column. Entries should be in date order.
Supplier:	The supplier name should be entered in this column.
F:	The F stands for folio which is used to trace this entry in the company books. The folio here will usually be the initials of the purchases ledger (PL) as that is where this posting will appear. The folio is usually inserted when the entry is being posted to the ledger and may also contain a number which references that particular account in the purchases ledger.
Inv./Cr. Note Number:	This column contains the invoice or credit note number as displayed on the invoice or credit note.
Total:	The gross total amount on the invoice/credit note including VAT should be recorded in this column.
Net Amounts:	Goods which are purchased to be resold later are categorised as Goods for Resale. Goods for resale may be purchased at more than one VAT rate and a separate column would be used for each separate VAT rate. The net amount of the goods is recorded in the appropriate column.

Alternatively, goods may be purchased for use in the running of the business. These goods include electricity, telephone, fixture and fittings, etc.. These goods are categorised as Goods Not for Resale. Goods not for resale may also be purchased at more than one VAT rate and a separate column would be used for each separate VAT rate. We will be using only one rate for non-resale so the net amount of the goods is entered in the column Goods Not for Resale.

There may be two, three or more columns used to record the net amount of goods at various VAT rates. These amounts are normally totalled on the invoice, but if not then it is a simple matter of totalling the net amounts at the various VAT rates from each line to the invoice.

VAT Amount: This column records the total VAT amount as shown on the invoice or credit note.

Analysis: The analysis columns are used to group the purchase of various items into categories which the management of the company require to be categorised as one group. The net amount of the goods recorded on the invoice or credit note are then entered in the appropriate analysis column.

When you have completed this task your daybook should look like the following:

Company Name: J.P. Murphy Electric

Purchases/Purchases Returns Daybook   **Month:** January ##

Date	Supp.	F	Inv./Cr. Note Number	Total	Goods for Resale Net @ 20%	Net @ 12.5%	Goods N for R Net @ 20%	VAT Amnt.	Purch.	Elec.	Tel.	Fix./Fit.
02/01/##	Solon Int.		216457	€6336.00	€5280.00	—	—	€1056.00	€5280.00	—	—	—

Task M-8

Enter the Purchase Invoices on Source Documents pages 11–12 into the Purchases/Purchases Returns Daybook.

Task M-9

Enter the Purchase Credit Note on Source Documents page 13 into the Purchases/Purchases Returns Daybook

The entry of the credit note is exactly the same as the entry of the invoice with the exception that all the money amounts must be recorded as minus amounts. This is done by placing a minus sign in front of each amount or by placing the amount in brackets. In recording figures it is very easy to fail to notice a minus in front of a number and therefore it is common practice in accounting to place the amount in brackets to indicate a minus amount. It is also a good idea to use a different colour for the recording of credit notes, however it should be clearly understood that the colour of the entry has no significance.

 NOTE: *1. In the case of Credit Notes the amounts are recorded as minus values by placing a minus sign in front of the figure or by placing the figure in brackets.*

2. The entries in the Purchases/Purchases Returns Daybook must be subsequently posted to the correct ledger accounts. The posting of these entries will be explained later.

Completed Purchases/Purchases Returns Daybook for January after entering transactions

Company Name: J.P. Murphy Electric

Purchases/Purchases Returns Daybook   **Month:** January ##

Date	Supp.	F	Inv./Cr. Note Number	Total	Goods for Resale Net @ 20%	Net @ 12.5%	Goods N for R Net @ 20%	VAT Amnt.	Purch.	Elec.	Tel.	Fix./Fit.
02/01/##	Solon Int.		216457	€6336.00	€5280.00	—	—	€1056.00	€5280.00	—	—	—
03/01/##	Philem Ire.		78542	€2376.00	€1980.00	—	—	€396.00	€1980.00	—	—	—
12/01/##	Mod. Com			€66.90	—	—	€55.75	€11.15	—	—	€55.75	—
13/01/##	Solon Int.		5347	(€158.40)	(€132.00)	—	—	(€26.40)	(€132.00)	—	—	—

(Analysis →)

 NOTE: *The folio (F) reference (PL in this case) is usually not entered until the figures are transferred to the ledger.*

Summary Note

Purchase Invoices and Credit Notes are entered in the Purchases/Purchases Returns

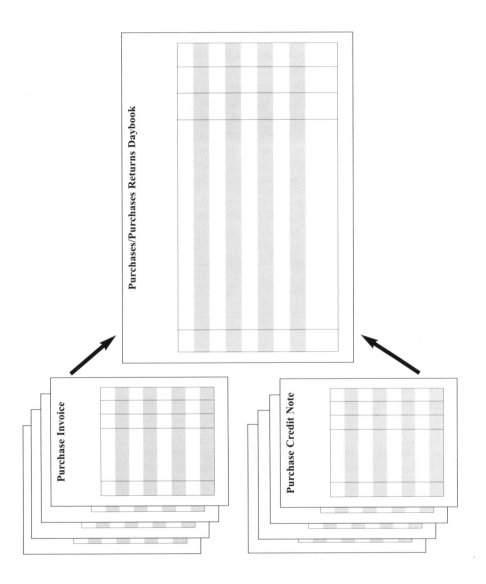

Cash (Bank) Payments Book

In the running of any business all monies paid out must be accurately recorded. The Cash (Bank) Payments Book is used to record all payments made by the company. Payments are normally made by writing a cheque, by direct debit (DD) or standing order (SO) and drawn on their bank account. Payments to suppliers normally have a remittance advice attached to the cheque and it is the remittance advice which is used as the source document in this book.

The Cash (Bank) Payments Book is the fourth daybook which we will be using. All payments should be recorded separately, with each individual payment occupying a single line in the Cash (Bank) Payments Book. The number of analysis columns may vary greatly from one business to another depending on the way in which the business wants its payments analysed, but each entry in the daybook will have an amount in at least one analysis column.

Another method used to record payments is an analysed cash book but this method will not be explained in this book.

We will now continue our work with the next task. You will require a Cash (Bank) Payments Book (sheet – Source Documents page 105) in order to perform this task.

Task M-10

Enter the details from the remittance advice on Source Documents page 14 into the Cash (Bank) Payments Book.

This task requires you to enter the details from the remittance advice into the Cash (Bank) Payments Book. The source document in this case is the remittance advice which is sent with the cheque to the supplier.

The entries in the Cash (Bank) Payments Book are as follows:

Date:	The date of the Payment should be entered in this column. This is normally the date on the remittance advice or the date of the DD or SO.
Details:	The details of this Payment, such as the suppliers name or what the payment is for (e.g. salaries, rent).
Cheque No.:	The cheque number for this payment. In the case of a direct debit the letters DD are entered and in the case of a standing order the letters SO are entered.
F:	This stands for folio and is the ledger reference for tracing this posting in company books. The folio will usually be PL (purchases ledger) as the majority of payments will be to suppliers. The folio for DDs and SOs will usually be NL (nominal ledger) as these will not generally be payments to suppliers. The folio is usually inserted when the entry is being posted to the ledger and may also contain a number which references that particular account in the sales ledger. Posting to ledgers will be explained later.

Total:	The amount of the cheque, DD or SO will be entered here.
Creditor:	If the payment is to a supplier (creditor) then the amount is entered under the Creditors column.
Salaries:	If the payment is for salaries then the amount is entered under the Salaries column.
Rent:	If the payment is for Rent then the amount is entered under the Rent column.
Petty Cash:	If the payment is a cheque which has been cashed to restore the petty cash imprest then the amount is entered under the Petty Cash column.
Other:	If the payment is for any purpose other than to a creditor or for salaries or rent or petty cash then the amount is entered under the Other column. Any entry in this column will have a note in the side margin explaining what the payment is for.

When you have completed this task the Cash (Bank) Payments Book should look like the following:

Company Name: J.P. Murphy Electric

Cash (Bank) Payments Book   **Month:** January ##

Date	Details	Cheque No.	F	Total	Analysis				
					Creditors	Salaries	Rent	Petty Cash	Other
23/01/##	Philem Ireland	200101		€2376.00	€2376.00	—	—	—	—

Task M-11

Enter the details from the remittance advice on Source Documents page 15 into the Cash (Bank) Payments Book.

Task M-12

A direct debit of €325.00 was made for Rent on 30/01/##. Enter this payment into the Cash (Bank) Payments Book.

The entry of this payment is exactly the same as a payment to a supplier, except that the analysis is entered in the Rent column and not the Creditors column.

NOTE: *The entries in the Cash (Bank) Payments Book must be subsequently posted to the correct ledger account. The posting of these entries will be explained later.*

Cash (Bank) Payments Book for January after entering transactions

Company Name: J.P. Murphy Electric

Cash (Bank) Payments Book   **Month:** January ##

| Date | Details | Cheque No. | F | Total | ←———— Analysis ————→ | | | | |
					Creditors	Salaries	Rent	Petty Cash	Other
23/01/##	Philem Ireland	200101		€2376.00	€2376.00	—	—	—	—
27/01/##	Solon International	200102		€6177.60	€6177.60	—	—	—	—
30/01/##	Rent Payment	DD		€325.00	—	—	€325.00	—	—

NOTE: *The folio (F) reference (PL and NL in this case) is usually not entered until the figures are transferred to the ledger.*

Summary Note

Remittance Advices and other Bank Payments are entered in the Cash (Bank) Payments Book

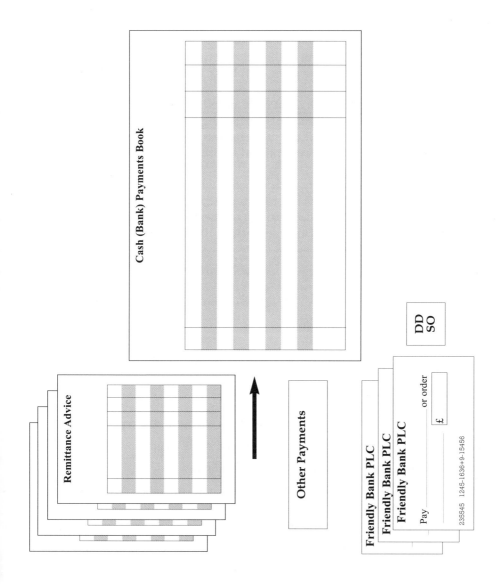

Petty Cash Book

Every business requires the purchase of small items, usually on a daily basis. It is not practical to issue an order for such items, receive an invoice and process the payment for them in the same way as for large items. It is also not practical to write a cheque for such small amounts.

Businesses normally retain a small amount of cash referred to as petty cash for the purchase of small items. The amount of this cash, at the start of each period, is referred to as the petty cash imprest and the petty cash book is used to record all items which are purchased using this cash.

All monies paid out of petty cash must be recorded on petty cash vouchers or dockets which are used as the source documents for writing up the petty cash book. The VAT on such items is often not recorded, but if a business wishes to reclaim the VAT then they must obtain a receipt for the payment, and record the VAT when entering the payment.

The source document is the petty cash voucher which is used when recording the payment. Each petty cash voucher is recorded on a separate row of the petty cash book.

We will now proceed with the task of writing up the petty cash book. You will require a Petty Cash Book (sheet – Source Documents page 105) in order to perform this task.

Task M-13

Enter the first petty cash voucher on Source Documents page 16 into the Petty Cash Book.

This task requires you to enter the details from the petty cash voucher into the Petty Cash Book.

The petty cash book uses the following columns:

Date:	Enter the date of the purchase, which should be the date on the voucher.
Expenditure:	Enter the details of the item(s) purchased in this column.
Voucher:	Enter the voucher number for the expenditure.
Total:	Enter the total amount of the expenditure (including VAT where this is recorded).
VAT:	Enter the VAT amount if applicable.
Analysis:	Enter the breakdown of the items purchased into the appropriate analysis columns, e.g. – post, – stationery, – cleaning, – miscellaneous expenses (anything that does not fit into any of the other analysis columns).

When you have completed this task the petty cash book should look like the following:

Company Name: J.P. Murphy Electric									

Petty Cash Book   Month: January ##

Date	Expenditure	Voucher No.	F	Total	VAT	Post	Stationery	Cleaning	Misc, Exp.
							← Analysis →		
05/01/##	Envelopes	1		€4.00	–	–	€4.00	–	–

Task M-14

Enter the remaining petty cash vouchers on Source Documents pages 16–18 into the Petty Cash Book.

NOTE: *The entries in the Petty Cash Book must be subsequently posted to the correct ledger account. The posting of these entries will be explained later.*

Completed Petty Cash Book for January after entering transaction

Company Name: J.P. Murphy Electric									

Petty Cash Book   Month: January ##

Date	Expenditure	Voucher No.	F	Total	VAT	Post	Stationery	Cleaning	Misc, Exp.
							← Analysis →		
05/01/##	Envelopes	1		€4.00	–	–	€4.00	–	–
09/01/##	Replace Window Glass	2		€16.88	€1.88	–	–	–	€15.00
11/01/##	Postage Stamps	3		€12.00	–	€12.00	–	–	–
13/01/##	Window Cleaning	4		€5.00	–	–	–	€5.00	–
17/01/##	Box of Pens	5		€9.50	–	–	€9.50	–	–

Summary Note

Petty Cash Vouchers are entered in the Petty Cash Book

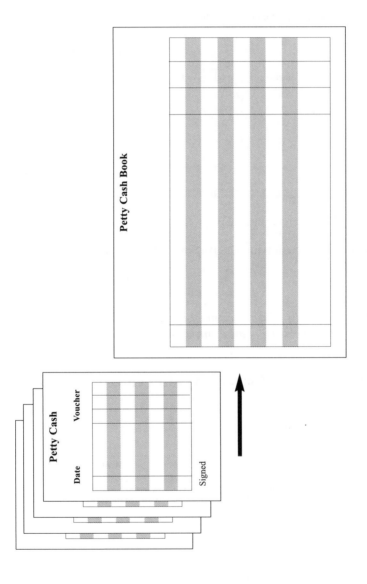

General Journal

The general journal is the sixth and final daybook. It is used to record any receipts or payments which do not readily fit into any of the other daybooks, e.g. capital investment, sale of an asset on credit. Very often there are no source documents used when making entries in the general journal. Entries in the general journal will occupy at least two rows. There will be at least one entry in the Debit column and at least one entry in the Credit column, with the total of both columns being equal. The number of entries in each column does not matter as long as the totals are equal. This is the essence of double entry which will be explained later. We will use the general journal to record the capital investment in a company.

The general journal is also used to record any internal bookkeeping which may need to be performed from time to time, e.g. accruals, prepayments. We will not be dealing with these in this book.

We will now proceed with the next task. In order to perform this task you should have a General Journal (sheet – Source Documents page 107).

Task M-15

J.P. Murphy commenced business on 01/01/## with a capital investment of €15,000.00. €14,900.00 of this was deposited in their current bank account and €100.00 was placed in petty cash. Use the General Journal to record these entries.

There are no source documents used in the recording of these entries. The information is contained in the task and will require three rows in the general journal. The general journal uses the following columns:

Date:	Enter the date of the transaction.
Details:	Enter the details of this transaction. The details should be sufficient to identify the Nominal Ledger account to be posted to.
F:	The folio will be Nominal Ledger (NL) as the entries in the general journal will be posted directly into the Nominal Ledger. The folio is usually inserted when the entry is being posted to the ledger and may also contain a number which references that particular account in the nominal ledger.
Debit:	Enter the debit amount for this entry if appropriate.
Credit:	Enter the credit amount for this entry if appropriate.
	It is normal practice to add an explanation on the next line of the general journal explaining the entry in the journal.

When you have completed this task the General Journal should look like the following:

Company Name: J.P. Murphy Electric

General Journal   **Month:** January ##

Date	Details	F	Debit	Credit
01/01/##	Bank Current A/C		€14,900.00	—
01/01/##	Petty Cash		€100.00	—
01/01/##	Capital		—	€15,000.00
	(Capital investment lodged)			

The entry of this capital investment requires the use of three rows in the general journal.

1. The first entry is the record of the money lodged to the bank current account. This entry will be posted to the Bank Current Account in the Nominal Ledger. Since the Bank Account is a Debit account (which will be explained later), any monies lodged to the bank are recorded on the debit side of the journal.

2. The second entry is the record of the money retained in petty cash. This entry will be posted to the Petty Cash Account in the Nominal Ledger. Since the Petty Cash Account is a bank account, then this entry will be on the debit side of the journal.

3. The third entry in the record of the capital which was invested in the company. This entry will be posted to the Capital Account in the Nominal (General) Ledger. Since the Capital account is a credit account (which will be explained later) then this entry is entered in the Credit side of the journal.

   The posting is usually completed by entering an explanation on the next line of the general journal.

Month End Calculations

The first task to be performed at the end of each month is to calculate the amount which was spent from petty cash and to restore the imprest to the correct amount. The company decides how much money should be in petty cash at the start of each month. This amount is called the imprest and therefore it must be restored at the end of each month before the month end calculations are performed. The petty cash imprest is restored from the bank current account, usually by cashing a cheque for the amount which was spent the previous week or month.

This cheque is recorded in the Cash (Bank) Payments Book in the same way as any other payment and is detailed as 'Restore Petty Cash Imprest'. The payment is analysed under the Petty Cash column. This will usually be the last entry in the Cash (Bank) Payments Book each month.

Task M-16

On the 31/01/## cheque number 200103 was cashed to restore the petty cash imprest. Calculate the amount of this cheque and enter it into the Cash (Bank) Payments Book.

Completed Cash (Bank) Payments Book for January

Company Name: J.P. Murphy Electric

Cash (Bank) Payments Book

Month: January ##

| Date | Details | Cheque No. | F | Total | Analysis | | | | |
					Creditors	Salaries	Rent	Petty Cash	Other
23/01/##	Philem Ireland	200101	PL	€2376.00	€2376.00	—	—	—	—
27/01/##	Solon International	200102	PL	€6177.60	€6177.60	—	—	—	—
30/01/##	Rent Payment	DD	NL	€325.00	—	—	€325.00	—	—
31/01/##	Restore Petty Cash Imprest	200103	NL	€47.38	—	—	—	€47.38	—

At the end of each month the columns in the daybooks which contain money amounts are totalled and cross checked to ensure accuracy and for posting to the ledgers.

Task M-17

Total all the daybooks and cross check the figures.

Cross checking of the day books should be performed as follows:

Sales/Sales Returns Daybook
> This book is cross checked as follows:

	Total Net Amount @ 20%
+	Total Net Amount @12.5%
+	Total VAT Amount
=	Total of Total column

A second crosscheck is:

	Total Sales
+	Total Repairs
+	Total VAT Amount
=	Total of Total column

Purchases/Purchases Returns Daybook
> This book is cross checked as follows:

	Total Goods for Resale
+	Total Goods Not for Resale
+	Total VAT Amount
=	Total of Total column

A second cross check is:

	Total Purchases
+	Total Electricity
+	Total Telephone
+	Total Fixture & Fittings
+	Total VAT Amount
=	Total of Total column

Cash Receipts (Bank Lodgement) Book
> This book is cross checked as follows:

	Total Cash Sales
+	Total Debtors
+	Total Other
=	Total of Total column

Cash (Bank) Payments Book
This book is cross checked as follows:

	Total Creditors
+	Total Salaries
+	Total Rent
+	Total Petty Cash
+	Total Other
=	Total of Total column

Petty Cash Book
This book is cross checked as follows:

	Total Post
+	Total Stationery
+	Total Cleaning
+	Total Miscellaneous Expenses
+	Total VAT
=	Total of Total column

Completed Daybooks

Company Name: J.P. Murphy Electric

Sales/Sales Returns Daybook   **Month:** January ##

Date	Customer	F	Inv./Cr. Note Number	Total	Net Amount @ 20%	@ 12.5%	VAT Amount	← Analysis → Sales	Repairs
06/01/##	James Mahon	SL	1001	€453.60	€378.00	—	€75.60	€378.00	—
07/01/##	The Electrical Shop	SL	1002	€1847.70	€1512.00	€29.60	€306.10	€1512.00	€29.60
09/01/##	New Age Contractors	SL	1003	€4952.85	€4058.00	€74.00	€820.85	€4058.00	€74.00
11/01/##	Cash Sale	SL	1004	€49.95	—	€44.40	€5.55	—	€44.40
12/01/##	Tomorrows Electronics	SL	1005	€4279.50	€3483.00	€88.80	€707.70	€3483.00	€88.80
13/01/##	New Age Contractors	SL	1006	(€549.60)	(€458.00)	—	(€91.60)	(€458.00)	—
			Totals:	€11034.00	€8973.00	€236.80	€1824.20	€8973.00	€236.80

Cash Receipts (Bank Lodgement) Book   **Month:** January ##

Date	Details	Lodge No.	F	Bank	Cash Sales	Debtors	Other
10/01/##	James Mahon (cheque 204587)	101	SL	€453.60	—	€453.60	—
11/01/##	Cash Sale	102	SL	€49.95	€49.95	—	—
21/01/##	The Electrical Shop (cheque 215687)	103	SL	€1847.70	—	€1847.70	—
22/01/##	New Age Contractors (cheque 272357)	104	SL	€4403.25	—	€4403.25	—
25/01/##	Tomorrows Electronics (cheque 467832)	105	SL	€4000.00	—	€4000.00	—
	Totals:			€10754.50	€49.95	€10704.55	€0.00

Purchases/Purchases Returns Daybook   **Month:** January ##

Date	Supp.	F	Inv./Cr. Note Number	Total	Goods for Resale Net @ 20%	Net @ 12.5%	Goods N for R Net @ 20%	VAT Amnt.	Purch.	Elec.	Tel.	Fix./Fit.
02/01/##	Solon Int.		216457	€6336.00	€5280.00	—	—	€1056.00	€5280.00	—	—	—
03/01/##	Philem Ire.		78542	€2376.00	€1980.00	—	—	€396.00	€1980.00	—	—	—
12/01/##	Mod. Com.			€66.90	—	—	€55.75	€11.15	—	—	€55.75	—
13/01/##	Solon Int.		5347	(€158.40)	(€132.00)	—	—	(€26.40)	(€132.00)	—	—	—
			Totals:	€8620.50	€7128.00	€0.00	€55.75	€1436.75	€7128.00	€0.00	€55.75	€0.00

Company Name: J.P. Murphy Electric

Cash (Bank) Payments Book

Month: January ##

Date	Details	Cheque No.	F	Total	Creditors	Salaries	Rent	Petty Cash	Other
23/01/##	Philem Ireland	200101	PL	€2376.00	€2376.00	—	—	—	—
27/01/##	Solon International	200102	PL	€6177.60	€6177.60	—	—	—	—
30/01/##	Rent Payment	DD	NL	€325.00	—	—	€325.00	—	—
31/01/##	Restore Petty Cash Imprest	200103	NL	€47.38	—	—	—	€47.38	—
			Totals:	€8925.98	€8553.60	€0.00	€325.00	€47.38	€0.00

Petty Cash Book

Month: January ##

Date	Expenditure	Voucher No.	F	Total	VAT	Post	Stationery	Cleaning	Misc, Exp.
05/01/##	Envelopes	1		€4.00	—	—	€4.00	—	—
09/01/##	Replace Window Glass	2		€16.88	€1.88	—	—	—	€15.00
11/01/##	Postage Stamps	3		€12.00	—	€12.00	—	—	—
13/01/##	Window Cleaning	4		€5.00	—	—	—	€5.00	—
17/01/##	Box of Pens	5		€9.50	—	—	€9.50	—	—
			Totals:	€47.38	€1.88	€12.00	€13.50	€5.00	€15.00

General Journal

Month: January ##

Date	Details	F	Debit	Credit
01/01/##	Bank Current A/C		€14,900.00	—
01/01/##	Petty Cash		€100.00	—
01/01/##	Capital		—	€15,000.00
	(Capital investment lodged)			
		Totals:	€15,000.00	€15,000.00

3. Ledgers

L edgers are used to assemble all the details about one customer, supplier, income, expense, asset, iability and owner's equity in one place. The information from the daybooks will be posted to an individual account in the appropriate ledger. Each day-book is used for a single month and then a new daybook is started for the next month. In the case of ledgers, each customer, supplier, etc. requires a separate sheet, and the same sheet is used until it is full and then another one is added. The information for each ledger account is therefore continuous.

We will be using the continuous balance method as this is becoming more popular and is the method used in computerised bookkeeping, The continuous balance method calculates the balance in an account each time an entry is made in that account. With this method there is no further calculation required in order to determine an account balance.

Another method is known as the T account method, but this method is not covered in this book.

There are three ledgers used for posting the various daybooks to, namely:

Sales (Debtors') Ledger – Customer accounts

Purchases (Creditors') Ledger – Supplier accounts

Nominal (General) Ledger – Company Accounts, i.e. Income, Expenses, Assets, Liabilities and Owner's Equity

All ledgers, using the continuous balance method, have three columns for entering money amounts. These columns are Debit (Dr), Credit (Cr), and Balance (Bal). It is essential that you enter the amount into the correct column and use the correct method to calculate the balance as will be explained when dealing with each individual ledger.

Posting from the daybooks uses the double entry system. This means that every entry in the daybooks must be posted to two separate accounts in the ledgers. It must be posted once on the Debit side of an account and once on the Credit side of another account. In most cases the second posting will not be as an individual amount, but rather as a total from a daybook, but it is still being posted the second time.

An example of this double entry is when a sale is recorded to a customer. The sale is initially recorded in the sales daybook. This entry is subsequently posted on the Debit side of the customers account in the Sales Ledger. The double entry in this case is that the goods sold to this customer are posted as part of the Total Sales on the Credit side of the Sales account in the Nominal Ledger and the VAT on this sale is posted as part of the Total VAT on the Credit side of the VAT account in the Nominal Ledger. Therefore the sale is posted twice, once as a Debit and once as a Credit. All entries in the daybooks will be posted twice and you should be able to trace the double entry of all entries in the daybooks.

Sales (Debtors') Ledgers

The record of all invoices and credit notes issued to a customer are recorded in the sales daybook. All the receipts from customers are recorded in the cash receipts (bank lodgement) book. However, neither of these books indicates how much any individual customer owes or how much they bought over a period of time.

The Sales (Debtors) Ledger is used to keep a record of all credit customers (debtors). Most businesses will also have an account named 'Cash Sale' which is used to record all cash sales. This account is treated as if it were a single customer, with entries recorded in the same way as any individual customer. All the entries in the sales day book and the receipts from customers, recorded in the cash receipts book, are posted to the Sales Ledger. Each customer has a separate page (sheet) in the Sales Ledger where all the sales and receipts for that particular customer are recorded. (All cash sales will be entered into a single account called 'Cash Sales'). This then is the next level of recording sales in the company.

We will now continue our work by posting the entries in the Sales/Sales Returns Daybook to the Sales Ledger.

Task M-18

Post the first entry in the Sales/Sales Returns Daybook to the Sales Ledger.

You will require a sales ledger card (sheet – Source Documents page 108) for this task.

The information for this task is obtained from the sales/sales returns daybook. Entries in the daybook should be posted to the sales ledger in date order. It is normal to post the entries from the cash receipts book at the same time so that the dates will be in order for each customer, but we will leave this until later.

Date: This is the date of the Invoice, Credit Note or receipt as entered in the daybook.

Details: The details of the entry in the ledger, e.g.

- Sales   Entry from the sales daybook. This entry may also contain the invoice number.

- Returns Entry from the sales returns daybook. This entry may also contain the credit note number.

- Receipt Entry of receipt from the cash receipts book. This entry may also contain the cheque number.

F: This stands for folio and is the reference for this posting in the ledger. The folio indicates where this posting originated, e.g.

- SB   Sales/Sales Returns **B**ook

- CRB   Cash Receipts (Bank Lodgement) **B**ook

The folio is usually inserted when the entry is being posted to the ledger. The folio in the daybook is usually inserted at the same time.

Dr: This stands for Debit and is the Debit amount of this posting. This is nearly always a sale. The amount is the total amount from the Total column in the daybook.

   Note: *Debit Sales in a Sales Ledger account*

Cr: This stands for Credit and is the Credit amount of this posting. This is usually either returns or a receipt of money. The amount is the total amount from the Total column in the daybook.

   Note: *Credit Receipts & Returns in a Sales Ledger account*

Bal: This stands for balance and is the running balance for this account. The balance is usually positive and is the amount that this customer owes us. It is calculated each time an entry is made in the ledger as follows:

   Bal = Previous Bal + Dr – Cr

   The Sales Ledger has a number of columns as follows:

In the Sales Ledger :

  Debits (Dr) are Positive +

  Credits (Cr) are Negative –

When you have completed this task, James Mahon's Sales Ledger should look like the following:

Company Name: J.P. Murphy Electric

Sales (Debtors) Ledger   **Debtor (Customer):** James Mahon

Date	Details	F	Debit	Credit	Balance
06/01/##	Sales (Invoice 1001)	SB	€453.60	—	€453.60

Task M-19

Post the remaining entries in the Sales/Sales Returns Daybook to the Sales Ledger.

You will require a number of sales ledger cards (sheet – Source Documents page 108) for this task.

When a credit note is being posted the amount is posted in the Cr column. The amount is not placed in brackets as the Cr column is a minus column in the sales ledger. The detail for a credit note would normally be Returns (credit note no. #####).

When all the individual entries in the Sales/Sales Returns Daybook have been posted it is normal practice to post the totals to the nominal ledger, thereby completing the double entry. However since we have not dealt with the nominal ledger yet we will leave that task until later.

Task M-20

Post the first entry in the Cash Receipts (Bank Lodgement) Book to the Sales Ledger.

The information for this task is obtained from the Cash Receipts (Bank Lodgement) Book. The posting of the receipts from the cash receipts book is exactly the same as posting the Sales and Returns. Post the individual entries from the cash receipts book to the Credit column of the customers account in the Sales Ledger. Receipt amounts are posted in the credit column because they must be subtracted from the amount this customer owes the company.

Again it is normal practice to post the totals to the nominal ledger, thereby completing the double entry, but we will leave this until we are dealing with the Nominal Ledger.

When you have completed this task, James Mahon's Sales Ledger should look like the following:

Company Name: J.P. Murphy Electric

Sales (Debtors) Ledger **Debtor (Customer):** James Mahon

Date	Details	F	Debit	Credit	Balance
06/01/##	Sales (Invoice 1001)	SB	€453.60	—	€453.60
10/01/##	Receipt (cheque 204587)	CRB	—	€453.60	€0.00

Task M-21

Post the remaining entries in the Cash Receipts (Bank Lodgement) Book to the Sales Ledger.

Completed Sales Ledgers

Company Name: J.P. Murphy Electric

Sales (Debtors) Ledger   **Debtor (Customer):** James Mahon

Date	Details	F	Debit	Credit	Balance
06/01/##	Sales (Invoice 1001)	SB	€453.60	–	€453.60
10/01/##	Receipt (cheque no 204587)	CRB	–	€453.60	€0.00

Sales (Debtors) Ledger   **Debtor (Customer):** The Electrical Shop

Date	Details	F	Debit	Credit	Balance
07/01/##	Sales (Invoice 1002)	SB	€1847.70	–	€1847.70
21/01/##	Receipt (cheque no 215687)	CRB	–	€1847.70	€0.00

Sales (Debtors) Ledger   **Debtor (Customer):** New Age Contractors

Date	Details	F	Debit	Credit	Balance
09/01/##	Sales (Invoice 1003)	SB	€4952.85	–	€4952.85
13/01/##	Returns (credit note 1006)	SB	–	€549.60	€4403.25
22/01/##	Receipt (cheque no 272357)	CRB	–	€4403.25	€0.00

Sales (Debtors) Ledger   **Debtor (Customer):** Cash Sale

Date	Details	F	Debit	Credit	Balance
11/01/##	Sales (Invoice 1004)	SB	€49.95	–	€49.95
11/01/##	Receipt (Cash)	CRB	–	€49.95	€0.00

Sales (Debtors) Ledger   **Debtor (Customer):** Tomorrows Electronics

Date	Details	F	Debit	Credit	Balance
12/01/##	Sales (Invoice 1005)	SB	€4279.50	–	€4279.50
25/01/##	Receipt (cheque no 467832)	CRB	–	€4000.00	€279.50

Summary Note

Sales Summary from Source
Documents to Sales Ledger

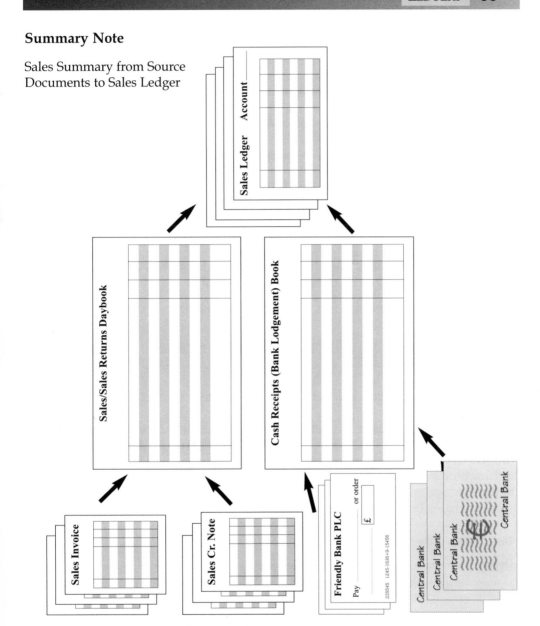

Purchases (Creditors') Ledgers

The record of all invoices and credit notes received from suppliers are recorded in the purchases daybook. All the payments made by the company are recorded in the cash (bank) payments book. However, neither of these books indicates how much the company owes any particular supplier or how much the company purchased from a supplier over a period of time.

The Purchases Ledger (Creditors Ledger) is used to keep a record of all suppliers (creditors). All the individual entries in the purchases day book and the payments made to suppliers, recorded in the cash (bank) payments book, are posted to the Purchases Ledger and the totals are posted to the Nominal Ledger. Each supplier has a separate page (sheet) in the Purchases Ledger where all the purchases and payments for that particular supplier are recorded. This then is the next level of recording purchases in the company.

We will now continue our work by posting the entries in the Purchases/Purchases Returns Daybook to the Purchases Ledger.

Task M-22

Post the first entry in the Purchases/Purchases Returns Daybook to the Purchases Ledger.

You will require a purchases ledger card (sheet – Source Documents page 109) for this task.

The information for this task is obtained from the purchases/purchases returns daybook. Entries in the daybook should be posted to the purchases ledger in date order. It is normal to post the entries from the 'Creditors' column in the cash payments book at the same time so that the dates will be in order for each supplier, but we will leave this until later.

The Purchases Ledger has a number of columns as follows:

Date:	This is the date of the Invoice, Credit Note or payment as entered in the daybook.

Details: The details of the entry in the ledger, e.g.

	– Purchases	Entry from the purchases daybook. This entry may also include an invoice number.
	– Returns	Entry from the purchases returns daybook. This entry may also include a credit note number.
	– Payment	Entry of Payment from the cash payments book. This entry may also include the cheque number.

F: This stands for folio and is the reference for this posting in the ledger. The folio indicates where this posting originated. e.g.

	– PB	Purchases/Purchases Returns Book
	– CPB	Cash (Bank) Payments Book

The folio is usually inserted when the entry is being posted to the ledger. The folio in the daybook is usually inserted at the same time.

Dr: This stands for Debit and is the Debit amount of this posting. This is nearly always a return or a payment. The amount is the total amount from the Total column in the daybook.

        Note: *Debit Payments & Returns* in a Purchases Ledger account

Cr: This stands for Credit and is the Credit amount of this posting. This is usually a purchase. The amount is the total amount from the Total column in the daybook.

        Note: *Credit Purchases* in a Purchases Ledger account

Bal: This stands for balance and is the running balance for this account. The balance is usually positive and is the amount that this customer owes us. It is calculated each time an entry is made in the ledger as follows:

        Bal = Previous Bal – Dr + Cr

NOTE: In the Purchases Ledger :

           Debits (Dr) are Negative –

           Credits (Cr) are Positive +

When you have completed this task, Solon International's, Purchases Ledger account should look like the following:

Company Name: J.P. Murphy Electric

Purchases (Creditors) Ledger   **Creditor (Supplier):** Solon International

Date	Details	F	Debit	Credit	Balance
02/01/##	Purchases (Invoice 216457)	PB	—	€6336.00	€6336.00

Task M-23

Post the remaining entries in the Purchases/Purchases Returns Daybook to the Purchases Ledger.

When a credit note is being posted the amount is posted in the Dr column. The amount is not placed in brackets as the Dr column is a minus column in the purchases ledger. The detail for a credit note would normally be Returns (credit note no. #####).

Task M-24

Post the first entry in the Cash (Bank) Payments Book to the Purchases Ledger.

The information for this task is obtained from the Cash (Bank) Payments Book. The posting of the payments from the cash payments book is exactly the same as posting the Purchases and Returns. Payment amounts are posted in the debit column because they must be subtracted from the amount the company owes this supplier.

When you have completed this task, Solon International Purchases Ledger account should look like the following:

Company Name: J.P. Murphy Electric

Purchases (Creditors) Ledger   Creditor (Supplier): Solon International

Date	Details	F	Debit	Credit	Balance
02/01/##	Purchases (Invoice 216457)	PB	—	€6336.00	€6336.00
13/01/##	Returns (Credit Note No: 5347)	PB	€158.40	—	€6177.60
27/01/##	Payment (cheque no: 200102)	CPB	€6177.60	—	€0.00

Task M-25

Post the remaining entries in the Cash (Bank) Payments Book to the Purchases Ledger.

Completed Purchases Ledgers

Company Name: J.P. Murphy Electric

Purchases (Creditors) Ledger **Creditor (Supplier):** Solon International

Date	Details	F	Debit	Credit	Balance
02/01/##	Purchases (Invoice 2164571)	PB	—	€6336.00	€6336.00
13/01/##	Returns (credit note no 5347)	PB	€158.40	—	€6177.60
27/01/##	Payment (cheque no 200102)	CPB	€6177.60	—	€0.00

Purchases (Creditors) Ledger **Creditor (Supplier):** Philem Ireland

Date	Details	F	Debit	Credit	Balance
03/01/##	Purchases (Invoice 78542)	PB	—	€2376.00	€2376.00
23/01/##	Payment (cheque no 200101)	CPB	€2376.00	—	€0.00

Purchases (Creditors) Ledger **Creditor (Supplier):** Modern Communications

Date	Details	F	Debit	Credit	Balance
12/01/##	Purchases	PB	—	€66.90	€66.90

Summary Note

Purchases Summary from
Source Documents to
Purchases Ledger

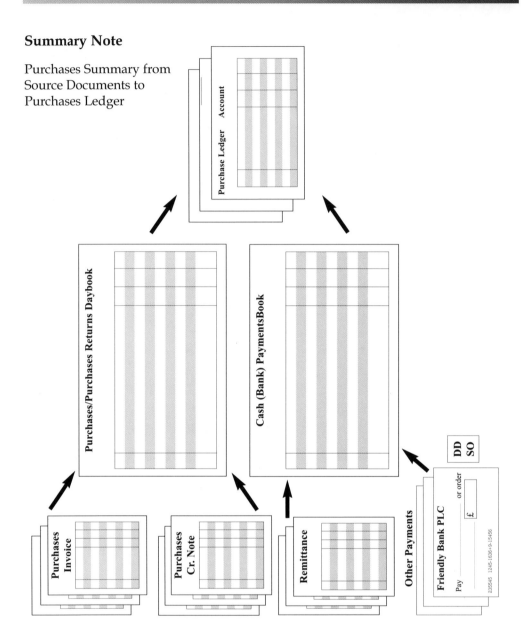

Nominal (General) Ledgers

The Nominal (General) Ledger consists of a number of accounts which are used to record the Income, Expenditure, Assets, Liabilities and Owner's Equity in the company. Every transaction which occurs in the company must eventually be recorded in the nominal ledger. Figures are transferred from the daybooks. The figures are normally posted on a monthly basis and are usually totals for the month as the individual figures will have already been entered in the sales or purchases ledgers. The balance figures in the nominal accounts are used in producing a Trial Balance which we will be doing later.

Nominal accounts will be one of five possible types Income, Expense, Asset, Liability or Owner Equity, as shown in the table below. Each type of account will be either a Debit (Dr) or Credit (Cr) account. This means that if an account is a Credit account then the balance in that account will normally be a Credit amount. If an account is a Debit account then the balance in that account will normally be a Debit amount. However a negative balance will result in a Debit account having a Credit balance instead of a Debit balance and vice versa.

Examples of Nominal Accounts:

Type	Dr or Cr	Examples
Income	Cr	When goods or services are sold by a company, the monies received are referred to as income and are recorded in an 'Income' account. Examples of income accounts are: Sales, Rent Received, Investment Income.
Expense	Dr	Any monies paid out by a business for the purchase of goods, materials or services required for the day-to-day running of the business are referred to as expenses and are recorded in an 'Expense' account. Examples of expense accounts are: Purchases, Electricity, Telephone, Rent Paid, Salaries Paid, Post, Stationary, Cleaning, Miscellaneous Expenses.
Asset	Dr	All items or monies which are owned by the business are regarded as asserts and are recorded in 'Asset' accounts. Examples of asset accounts are: Debtors, Bank, Petty Cash, Stock, Machinery, Fixtures & Fittings, Vehicles.
Liability	Cr	Any monies owed by a business at any time are referred to as liabilities and are recorded in a 'Liability' account. Examples of liability accounts are: Creditors, VAT payable, PRSI payable, Bank overdraft.
Owner Equity	Cr	All monies invested in a business and profits retained by the business are referred to as owner equity and are recorded in an 'Owner Equity' account. Examples of owner equity accounts are: Shares, Retained Profits.

Calculating the Balance in an Account

Every time an entry is made in an account then the Balance must be calculated in a similar manner to the sales and purchases ledger. However in the case of the nominal ledger some accounts are credit accounts and some accounts are debit accounts. This means that before you calculate the balance you must firstly ascertain if the account is a debit or credit account. The various account types are shown in the above table.

In the case of Debit accounts – Debits are positive (+) and Credits are Negative (–)

In the case of Credit accounts – Credits are positive (+) and Debits are Negative (–)

Writing Up the Nominal (General) Ledger

The writing up of the Nominal Ledger is very similar to the Sales and Purchase Ledger and we will be using the continuous balance method. However, the T account method is also in common use.

The Nominal Ledger has a number of columns into which entries should be made as follows:

Date:	The date of the entry in the ledger. This is usually the last day of the month.
Details:	The details of the entry in the ledger.
F:	F stands for folio and is the reference for this posting in the ledger, i.e. where this posting came from.
Dr:	If the account is a Debit account then the posting will normally have an entry in the Debit column.
Cr:	If the account is a Credit account then the posting will normally have an entry in the Credit column.
Bal:	This is the running balance for the account. The balance is usually positive and will be a Debit or Credit amount depending on the type of account. However a negative balance will be indicated by placing the figure in brackets as in the daybooks and usually writing the letters Dr or Cr in the right margin to indicate that the balance is opposite to the type of account.

We will now proceed with the task of writing up the Nominal (General) Ledger Accounts. You will need a number of nominal ledger cards (sheet – Source Documents page 110) for this task.

Task M-26

Post the figures from the General Journal into the Nominal (General) Ledger.

This is the easiest daybook to transfer figures from as the figures are already written in the correct columns. When posting from the general journal Debits are posted as Debits in the nominal ledger and Credits are posted as Credits in the nominal ledger.

The first entry we will post from the general journal is Capital. This means that we need a Capital Account.

When this entry is made the Nominal (General) Ledger - Capital Account should look like the following:

Company Name: J.P. Murphy Electric

Nominal (General) Ledger   Nominal Account: Capital

Date	Details	F	Debit	Credit	Balance
31/01/##	Capital Investment	GJ	–	€15000.00	€15000.00

The second entry we will post is the Bank Current A/C so we need a Bank Current A/C account.

When this entry is made the Nominal (General) Ledger – Bank Current A/C account should look like the following:

Company Name: J.P. Murphy Electric

Nominal (General) Ledger   Nominal Account: Bank Current A/C

Date	Details	F	Debit	Credit	Balance
31/01/##	Capital Investment	GJ	€14900.00	–	€14900.00

The third entry we will post is to Petty Cash. This is entered in the Petty Cash Account in the same way as the above.

We will now continue with the task of posting the Sales/Sales Returns Daybook to the Nominal (General) Ledger.

Task M-27

Post the totals from the Sales/Sales Returns Daybook into the Nominal (General) Ledger.

The following totals must be posted to the Debit or Credit columns of the individual nominal accounts:

Sales Total   The sales account is a Credit Account so the Sales total is simply posted to the Cr column of the Sales Account.

Repairs Total   The repairs account is a Credit Account so the Repairs total is simply posted to the Cr column of the Repairs Account.

VAT Total   The VAT payable account is a Credit account as it is a liability account and will normally have a Credit balance. However it is one of the accounts which will have entries in both the Debit and Credit columns. The VAT total from the Sales/Sales Returns Daybook is posted in the Credit column as this is the VAT which is collected and is due to be paid to the collector general.

When you have completed this task the Sales Account in the Nominal (General) Ledger should look like the following:

Company Name: J.P. Murphy Electric					
Nominal (General) Ledger				**Nominal Account:** Sales	
Date	**Details**	**F**	**Debit**	**Credit**	**Balance**
31/01/##	Sales (January ##)	SDB	–	€8973.00	€8973.00

The Repairs and VAT accounts will look similar to the Sales account.

NOTE: *The individual rows of the Sales/Sales Returns Daybook have already been posted to the individual debtors accounts in the Sales Ledger. This means that every entry in the sales/sales returns daybook has been posted to two ledger accounts, once on the Debit side and once on the Credit side.*

The next task is to post the Purchases/Purchases Returns Daybook to the Nominal (General) Ledger.

Task M-28

Post the totals from the Purchases/Purchases Returns Daybook to the Nominal (General) Ledger.

The following totals must be posted to the Debit or Credit columns of the individual nominal accounts:

Purchases Total   The purchases account is a Debit Account so the Purchases total is simply posted to the Dr column of the Purchases Account.

Electricity Total   The Electricity account is a Debit Account so the Electricity total is simply posted to the Dr column of the Electricity Account. Since there was no entry in the Electricity column you may skip this account until next month.

Telephone Total   The Telephone account is a Debit Account so the Telephone total is simply posted to the Dr column of the Telephone Account.

Fixture & Fittings   The Fixture & Fittings account is a Debit Account so the Fixture & Fittings total is simply posted to the Dr column of the Fixture & Fittings Account. Since there was no entry in the Fixture & Fittings column you may skip this account until next month.

VAT Total   The VAT payable account is a Credit account as it is a liability account and will normally have a Credit balance. However when posting from the Purchases/Purchases Returns Daybook the amount is posted in the *Debit* column as this is VAT which the company has paid out and which it is reclaiming from the collector general. This amount is subtracted from the previous balance amount in order to obtain the Balance figure.

When you have completed this task the Purchases Account in the Nominal (General) Ledger should look like the following:

Company Name: J.P. Murphy Electric

Nominal (General) Ledger   **Nominal Account:** Purchases

Date	Details	F	Debit	Credit	Balance
31/01/##	Purchases (January ##)	PDB	€7128.00	—	€7128.00

The Telephone Account will look similar to the Purchases Account.

The VAT account will now look like the following:

Company Name: J.P. Murphy Electric

Nominal (General) Ledger   **Nominal Account:** VAT Payable

Date	Details	F	Debit	Credit	Balance
31/01/##	VAT on Sales (Jan ##)	SDB	—	€1824.20	€1824.20
31/01/##	VAT on Purchases (Jan ##)	PDB	€1436.75	—	€387.45

| NOTE: | *The individual rows of the Purchases/Purchases Returns Daybook have already been posted to the individual creditors accounts in the Purchase Ledger. This means that every entry in the purchases/purchases returns* |

daybook has been posted to two ledger accounts, once on the Debit side and once on the Credit side.

The next task is to post the Cash Receipts (Bank Lodgement) Book to the Nominal (General) Ledger.

Task M-29

Post the totals from the Cash Receipts (Bank Lodgement) Book to the Nominal (General) Ledger.

In this case the only figure which we need to post is the Total of the Bank column to the Bank Current A/C in the nominal ledger. This account is another account where entries are made in the Debit and Credit columns. The Bank Current Account is a Debit account and therefore the total from the Cash Receipts (Bank Lodgement) Book is posted to the Debit column as it is money received by the company.

The next task is to post the Cash (Bank) Payments Book to the Nominal (General) Ledger.

Task M-30

Post the totals from the Cash (Bank) Payments Book to the Nominal (General) Ledger.

The following totals must be posted to the Debit or Credit columns of the individual nominal accounts:

Total Total   The Total of all payments must be posted to the Bank Current A/C in the nominal ledger. Even though Bank Current A/C is a Debit account the total from the Cash (Bank) Payments Book is posted to the Credit column as it is money paid out by the company and therefore reduces the amount in the Bank.

Salaries Total   The Salaries account is a Debit Account so the Salaries total is simply posted to the Dr column of the Salaries Account. Since there was no entry in the Salaries column you may skip this account until next month.

Rent Total   The Rent account is a Debit Account so the Rent total is simply posted to the Dr column of the Rent Account.

Petty Cash Total   This is the money which has been transferred to Petty Cash to restore the imprest. The Petty Cash account is a Debit Account so the Petty Cash total is simply posted to the Dr column of the Petty Cash Account as this is money paid *into* petty cash, in the same way as money paid into the bank account is posted to the Debit side.

Other   Entries in this column would have a note written in the side margin indicating what the payment was for and the entry would then be posted to the relevant account. Since there was no entry in the Other column you may skip this account.

When you have completed this task the Bank Current A/C in the Nominal (General) Ledger should look like the following:

Company Name: J.P. Murphy Electric

Nominal (General) Ledger   **Nominal Account:** Bank Current A/C

Date	Details	F	Debit	Credit	Balance
31/01/##	Capital Investment	GJ	€14900.00	—	€14900.00
31/01/##	Bank Lodgements (Jan ##)	CRB	€10754.50	—	€25654.45
31/01/##	Cash Payments (Jan ##)	CPB	—	€8925.98	€16728.52

The final daybook to be posted to the Nominal (General) Ledger is the Petty Cash Book.

Task M-31

Post the totals from the Petty Cash Book to the Nominal (General) Ledger.

The following totals must be posted to the Debit or Credit columns of the individual nominal accounts

Total Total	The Total amount of petty cash payments for the period is posted to the Credit side of the Petty Cash Account. The Petty Cash account is a Debit Account but in the same way as payments out of the bank account are posted to the Credit side, so the payments out of petty cash are posted to the Cr column of the Petty Cash Account.
Post Total	The Post account is a Debit Account so the Post total is posted to the Dr column of the Post Account.
Stationery Total	The Stationery account is a Debit Account so the Stationery total is posted to the Dr column of the Stationery Account.
Cleaning Total	The Cleaning account is a Debit Account so the Cleaning total is posted to the Dr column of the Cleaning Account.
Misc. Exp. Total	The Miscellaneous Expenses account is a Debit Account so the Misc. Exp. total is posted to the Dr column of the Miscellaneous Expenses Account.
VAT Total	The VAT payable account is a Credit account as it is a liability account and will normally have a Credit balance. However when posting from the Petty Cash book the amount is posted in the *Debit* column, in the same way as VAT on purchase is entered, as this is VAT which the company has paid out and which it is reclaiming from the collector general. This amount is subtracted from the previous balance amount in order to obtain the Balance figure.

Completed Nominal ledgers

Company Name: J.P. Murphy Electric

Nominal (General) Ledger   **Nominal Account:** Sales

Date	Details	F	Debit	Credit	Balance
31/01/##	Sales (January ##)	SB	—	€8973.00	€8973.00

Nominal (General) Ledger   **Nominal Account:** Repairs

Date	Details	F	Debit	Credit	Balance
31/01/##	Repairs (January ##)	SB	—	€236.80	€236.80

Nominal (General) Ledger   **Nominal Account:** Purchases

Date	Details	F	Debit	Credit	Balance
31/01/##	Purchases (January ##)	PB	€7128.00	—	€7128.00

Nominal (General) Ledger   **Nominal Account:** Telephone

Date	Details	F	Debit	Credit	Balance
31/01/##	Telephone (January ##)	PB	€55.75	—	€55.75

Nominal (General) Ledger   **Nominal Account:** Rent

Date	Details	F	Debit	Credit	Balance
31/01/##	Rent (January ##)	CPB	€325.00	—	€325.00

Nominal (General) Ledger   **Nominal Account:** Post

Date	Details	F	Debit	Credit	Balance
31/01/##	Post (January ##)	PCB	€12.00	—	€12.00

Nominal (General) Ledger   **Nominal Account:** Stationery

Date	Details	F	Debit	Credit	Balance
31/01/##	Stationery (January ##)	PCB	€13.50	—	€13.50

Nominal (General) Ledger   **Nominal Account:** Cleaning

Date	Details	F	Debit	Credit	Balance
31/01/##	Cleaning (January ##)	PCB	€5.00	—	€5.00

Nominal (General) Ledger   **Nominal Account:** Misc. Expenses

Date	Details	F	Debit	Credit	Balance
31/01/##	Misc. Exp. (January ##)	PCB	€15.00	—	€15.00

Nominal (General) Ledger   **Nominal Account:** Bank Current A/C

Date	Details	F	Debit	Credit	Balance
01/01/##	Capital Investment	GJ	€14900.00	—	€14900.00
31/01/##	Bank Lodgements (Jan ##)	CRB	€10754.50	—	€25654.50
31/01/##	Cash Payments (Jan ##)	CPB	—	€8925.98	€16728.52

Nominal (General) Ledger   **Nominal Account:** Petty Cash

Date	Details	F	Debit	Credit	Balance
01/01/##	Opening Balance	GJ	€100.00	—	€100.00
31/01/##	Total Payments (Jan ##)	PCB	—	€47.38	€52.62
31/01/##	Restore Imprest	BPB	€47.38	—	€100.00

Nominal (General) Ledger   **Nominal Account:** VAT Payable

Date	Details	F	Debit	Credit	Balance
31/01/##	VAT on Sales (Jan ##)	SB	—	€1824.20	€1824.20
31/01/##	VAT on Purchases (Jan ##)	PB	€1436.75	—	€387.45
31/01/##	VAT on Petty Cash Purchases (Jan ##)	PCB	€1.88	—	€385.57

Nominal (General) Ledger   **Nominal Account:** Capital

Date	Details	F	Debit	Credit	Balance
01/01/##	Capital Investment	GJ	—	€15000.00	€15000.00

Summary Note

Totals from Daybooks are posted to the Nominal Ledger.

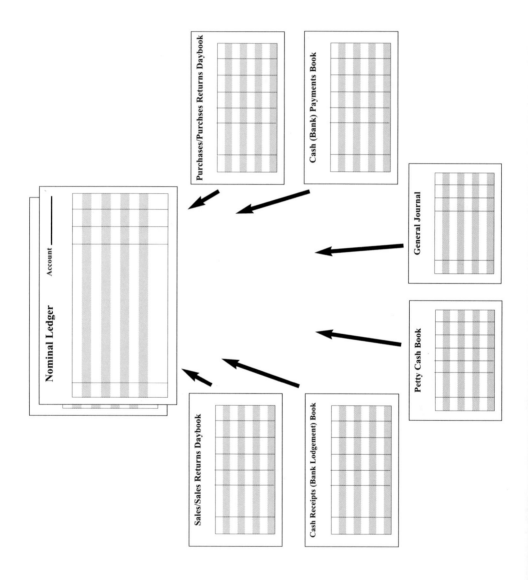

4. Trial Balance

At regular intervals, usually every month, a company will perform a trial balance. A trial balance is a list of all nominal accounts with the balance in each account listed. Where debtors' and creditors' control accounts are not used, the totals from the sales and purchase ledger are also included.

Since every transaction has been entered into two Ledger Accounts, once on the debit side and once on the credit side, then the total of all the debits should equal the total of all the credits. A trial balance is used to check that this is correct. A trial balance does not ensure that all entries are correct, it simply checks that the total of the debits equals the total of the credits. However, this procedure usually shows up any errors which have been made over the period since the last trial balance.

If a trial balance does not balance, i.e. the total of the debits does not equal the total of the credits, then the error may be corrected or a balancing amount posted to a suspense account and the correction made later. In any event the correction should be made before the next trial balance is performed.

Task M-32

Extract a trial balance from the books of J.P. Murphy Electric as at 31/01/##

The term "as at" means from the start of the financial year up to the stated date. In this case since we have only completed the first month, this will mean that there will only be one months figures in the trial balance.

Procedure for performing a Trial Balance

The figures for a trial balance is taken from the closing balances from all of the Nominal (General) Ledger accounts. The totals of the balances from the Sales Ledger accounts and Purchases Ledger accounts are also included in a trial balance. The nominal accounts are assembled by type, i.e. Income, Expense, Asset, Liability and Owner's Equity. A list is then made of all the accounts together with a debit and credit column, as shown below. An entry for Debtors and Creditors is also made. If the account is a Debit account then the balance figure is written in the Debit column, and if the account is a Credit account then the Balance figure is written in the Credit column (see page 41 for a list of account types). The total of the debtors (taken from the sales ledgers), is a Debit amount and the total of the creditors (taken from the purchases ledgers), is a Credit amount. Care should be taken that an account balance is not negative, as in such a case the balance figure is written in the opposite column.

The complete trial balance is shown below.

Company Name: J.P. Murphy Electric

Trial Balance as at 31/01/##

	Debit	Credit
Sales		€8973.00
Repairs		€236.80
Purchases	€7128.00	
Rent	€325.00	
Telephone	€55.75	
Post	€12.00	
Stationery	€13.50	
Cleaning	€5.00	
Miscellaneous Expenses	€15.00	
Debtors	€279.50	
Bank Current Account	€16728.52	
Petty Cash	€100.00	
Creditors		€66.90
VAT Payable		€385.57
Capital		€15000.00
	€24662.27	€24662.27

NOTE: *1. The Debtors' figure is the total of all the balance figures from the Sales (Debtors') Ledger.*

2. The Creditors' figure is the total of all the balance figures from the Purchases (Creditors') Ledger.

5. Completing the VAT 3 Form

Every company who is registered for VAT must make a return to the Collector General on a two monthly basis. This is done be completing a VAT 3 form which is sent to each company for the purpose of making a return. The VAT 3 form is preprinted with all the company information such as name, address, VAT number, etc. already on the form. The company has simply to calculate the amount of VAT collected and the amount paid out and enter these figures on the form. The amount to be paid to (or in some cases repaid from) the Collector General is then entered on the form.

> ## Task M-33
>
> Complete a VAT 3 form for the month of January ##

The necessary information for completing the VAT 3 form can be obtained from the VAT account in the Nominal (General) Ledger. The figures to be entered are as follows:

1. The VAT account is a Credit account, which means that the Balance figure is normally a Credit amount. In this case the Balance figure is the amount of VAT which has to be paid to the Collector General, and is entered in the T3 box on the form.

   However if the Balance figure is a Debit figure then the figure will be in brackets, in the Nominal Ledger, and will usually have the letters Dr in the right margin. This amount has to be repaid from the Collector General and is entered in the T4 box on the form.

2. The total VAT collected (VAT output) is the total of the Credit column, therefore this figure is entered in box T1 on the VAT 3 form.

3. The total VAT paid (VAT input) is the total of the Debit column therefore this figure is entered in box T2 on the VAT 3 form.

Company Name: J.P. Murphy Electric

Nominal (General) Ledger   Nominal Account: VAT Payable

Date	Details	F	Debit	Credit	Balance
31/01/##	VAT on Sales (Jan ##)	SB	—	€1824.20	€1824.20
31/01/##	VAT on Purchases (Jan ##)	PB	€1436.75	—	€387.45
31/01/##	VAT on Petty Cash Purchases (Jan ##)	PCB	€1.88	—	€385.57
			€1438.63	€1824.20	

T2   T1   **T3 if Credit / T4 if Debit**

In all correspondence please Quote

Registration No: IE **7584682P**

Notice No: 06334829-00040P

<small>67839 151968 67521 1511481 000312VAT3R0</small>

Office of the Revenue Commissioners
Collector-Generals Division
Sarsfield House
Francis Street
Limerick

Period: **01-01-##**
31-01-##

J. P. Murphy Electric
Main Street
Naas
Co. Kildare

Enquiries: 1800 203070

Payment due by:

VAT3 RETURN

Please print one figure only in each space using a black or blue ball point pen.

1. VAT

IR£ : ENTER PUNTS ONLY

VAT ON SALES *   T1   **1 8 2 4** ·00

OFFICE USE ONLY

AMD A1 ☐

O/S A2 ☐

VAT ON PURCHASES *   T2   **1 4 3 8** ·00

Net Repayable		OR		Net Payable	
T4	·00		I3	**3 8 6**	·00
(Excess of T2 over T1)				(Excess of T1 over T2)	

2. TRADING WITH OTHER EU COUNTRIES

Total goods to other EU countries   Total goods from other EU countries

E1   ·00   E2   ·00

3. BANK DETAILS FOR REPAYMENTS / REFUNDS

SORT CODE B1 ☐☐☐   ACCOUNT NUMBER B2 ☐☐☐☐☐☐

Only complete if you have not previously advised us of account details or you wish to amend previously submitted details. Any repayment of VAT will be repaid to the bank or building society account as notified.

I declare that this is a correct return of Value Added Tax for the period specified :-

Signed:- *<Student Name>*   Status:- *Student*   Date:- **31-01-##**

BANK GIRO
CREDIT TRANSFER

Revenue

To	BANK OF IRELAND COLLEGE GREEN DUBLIN 2	**90-71-04**	For	COLLECTOR-GENERAL VALUE ADDED TAX A/C NO. 31468191

Name: *J. P. Murphy Electric*
Period: **01-01-## – 31-01-##**

Registration No. IE **7584682P**

Notice No:

I declare that the amount shown below is the amount I am liable to remit to the Collector-General for the above period.

Signed: *<Student Name>*   Date: **31-01-##**

IR£

	IR£
CASH	
CHEQUES	**386 - 00**
TOTAL	**386 - 00**

VAT Payable	**386**	00

Whole Punts only. Please do not enter pence.

Receiving Cashier's Brand & Initials

Please do not fold this payslip or write or mark below this line.

VAT 3 IR£

⑉90⑉7104⑉ 31468191⑉ 80

6. Exercises M-1 and M-2

Exercise M-1

1. Write up the source documents on Source Documents pages 22–55 in the appropriate day books.

2. A direct debit of €1532.75 was made for Salaries on 28/02/##. Write up this transaction in the appropriate daybook.

3. Cheque number 200207 was cashed on 28/02/## to restore the petty cash imprest to €100.00. Calculate the amount of this cheque and enter it in the appropriate daybook.

4. Post the entries from all the daybooks to the appropriate ledger accounts.

5. Extract a trial balance as at the last day of February ##.

6. Complete a VAT 3 form for the months of January and February ##.

Exercise M-2

1. Gem Jewellers, Patricks Street, Cork commenced business on 01/01/## with a capital investment of €25000.00. €24800.00 of this was deposited in their current bank account and €200.00 was placed in petty cash. Use the General Journal to record these entries.

2. Write up the source documents on Source Documents pages 61–81 in the appropriate day books.

3. Write up the following Direct Debit payments into the appropriate day book:

   ● Rent Payment of €450.00 on 25/01/##

   ● Salary Payment of €1108.56 on 30/01/##

4. Cheque number 215014 was cashed on 31/01/## to restore the petty cash imprest to €200.00. Calculate the amount of this cheque and enter it in the appropriate daybook.

5. Post the entries from all the daybooks to the appropriate ledger accounts.

6. Extract a trial balance as at the last day of January ##.

7. Complete a VAT 3 form for the months of January ##.

PART II

COMPUTER PRINCIPLES

7. Computers

Computers have developed rapidly over the last 20 years. The pace of development continues at an ever increasing pace. It is therefore difficult to keep notes on computers up-to-date. However, there are certain principles which are basic and these will be explained in this section.

The simplest definition of a computer is: 'A computer is a machine for processing data.' It can process numeric and non numeric data. For example:

- A computer can take a list of names and sort them into alphabetical order.
- A computer can take information about worker's rates of pay, hours worked, PAYE/PRSI deductions, etc. and produce a weekly or monthly payroll.
- Computers are used to produce millions of letters and documents every day .
- Computers are also used to keep accounts, produce payrolls, run the lotto, play music, produce drawings, play games, guide aircraft, keep records, surf the internet, send/receive e-mail and numerous other tasks.

The computer cannot of course do these things on its own. People must supply the data, give exact instructions as to how it is to be processed and specify what results are required. Instructions are given to a computer by a program.

Main Parts of a Personal Computer

The main parts of a computer are shown in the diagram. These parts are:

1. Computer Housing, containing:
   (i) Central Processing Unit (CPU)
   (ii) Memory (RAM)
   (iii) Hard Disk
   (iv) CD ROM or DVD
   (v) Floppy Disk Drive
2. Monitor
3. Keyboard
4. Mouse

Personal Computer

Computer Housing

Computers as we have come to know them are generally housed on a case which sits on the desk (desktop) or stands on the ground (tower). The shape and size of the housing does not matter, what is important is what is inside. The following are the parts which make up a modern Personal Computer (PC).

Central Processing Unit

The central processing unit (CPU), commonly known as the microprocessor or the central processor is in effect the brain of the computer. It performs the task of organising the work of all the other components and also carries out arithmetic, sorting and other functions.

CPUs, which are often referred to as the 'chip', are developing at an ever increasing pace, with a new one being released practically every month, and a new generation nearly every year. The largest manufacturer of CPUs is Intel. At present the latest chip is an Intel Pentium IV, with a clock speed of 800 MHz. I am sure that by the time you are reading this there will be another generation on the market. Find out what chip is in the computer you are using.

CPU

Random Access Memory (RAM)

The random access memory is the computer's workspace where the program instructions and the data being worked on will reside. The CPU can read from and write to RAM. In most computers anything stored in RAM will be lost when the computer is switched off or in the event of a power failure and for this reason it is referred to as volatile memory.

The size of the RAM is very important as it controls the size of program which may be used on the computer and the speed at which it can process information. Most programs specify a minimum size RAM, below which the program will not function. However this size should be considered a minimum and the more RAM which a machine has the better will be the performance of the machine. Modern computers usually will have a minimum of 128 MB of RAM. Find out what size RAM is in the computer you are using.

RAM

Hard Disk

The hard disk is simply the storage space in the computer itself. The computer has very fast access to date/information stored on its hard disk. The size of the hard disk is important as modern programs are very extensive and take up a lot of space on the hard disk. The size of files generated by modern programs tend to be quite large and because of the number of files generated daily the hard disk needs to be quite large. Modern computers will usually have a hard disk size of about 20GB (i.e. 20,000 MB). Find out what size hard disk is in the computer you are using.

Hard Disk

CD ROM/DVD

Most programs are now supplied on CD ROM (Compact Disk – Read Only Memory). In order to install these programs it is necessary to have a CD ROM drive in a computer. Films are now being distributed on disk. This is also a Compact Disk but the way in which the data is stored on the disk is different to a standard CD. It is therefore necessary to have a DVD (Digital Video Disk) drive in a computer. A DVD drive will also read CD ROMs but a CD ROM will not read a DVD. Find out if there is a CD ROM or DVD fitted in the computer you are using.

CD ROM

Floppy Disk Drives

In order to transport information from one computer to another and to store a copy of information which is stored on the hard disk, there is a need for some secondary storage medium. The most common type of secondary storage is a Floppy Disk. These disks hold about 1.5 MB of data. In order to use these disks on a machine it is necessary to have a floppy disk drive in the computer housing. These disk drives are very slow, compared with a hard disk but they are very useful as a means of secondary storage.

Floppy Disk Drive

Monitor

The monitor is attached to the computer so that people can see what they are doing and what the computer is doing. Modern monitors are cathode ray tubes and are very clear. The clarity of slim-line monitors is improving at a very fast pace and they are becoming more and more popular, but the cost of these screens is still quite high. However before very long the slim-line will be the most popular.

The size of the screen is also important in order to see as much as possible on the screen without having to scroll over the display. The standard size monitor attached to modern computers is a 17-inch monitor, however larger sizes are also becoming more common Find out what size monitor is attached the computer you are using.

Slim-line Monitor

Standard Monitor

Keyboard

The keyboard is still the most common input device for a computer. However technology is progressing at an ever increasing pace and voice recognition is developing fast. It is possible to have your computer operate in response to your voice, but the training it quite long and tedious. However this will change rapidly and it may not be too long before we will have computers operating without a keyboard.

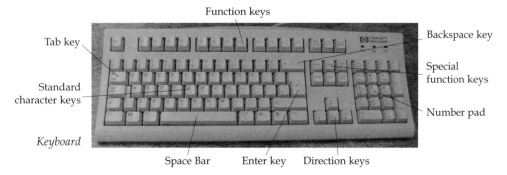

Function keys

Tab key

Standard character keys

Keyboard

Space Bar Enter key Direction keys

Backspace key

Special function keys

Number pad

Mouse

The mouse is a pointing device which is fitted to a computer to allow you to select items displayed on the screen. The mouse is used to make the operation of programs more user friendly. It is possible to operate most programs using the keyboard only, however, this is becoming increasingly more difficult with the complexities of modern programs.

Mouse

Hardware

This is the term used to describe all the electronic and mechanical elements of the computer. Hardware is basically something that has size and shape, and you can see and touch it. Examples of hardware would be: CPU, RAM, monitor, keyboard, printer, disk drive, disks (hard or floppy), mouse, cables, etc.

Programs

The computer cannot do anything on its own. It must be given very exact instructions which it will follow. These instructions are given to the computer by people and they are contained in what is known as a program. The activity of producing a program is called programming

A program may be only a few lines long or it may contain several thousand lines depending on what is required of it. Most programs in common use are written by specialists who are employed by software houses to do this job. Most people who use computers have some knowledge of programming, but this is not essential in order to operate a computer.

Software

This is the general term used to describe the various programs used on a computer. Software is something that has no size and you cannot touch it, but a computer can do nothing without it. Software is generally supplied on a CD ROM or floppy disk. It is in fact the programs stored on the disk which constitutes software.

Software can be divided into two categories, systems software and applications software. The systems software manages the computer while the applications software performs the tasks required by the person using the computer.

Software is normally supplied on CD or floppy disk and must be transferred to the hard disk on the computer in order to use it. This process is referred to as Installing or Setting Up the software. Another method of obtaining software, which is becoming more and more common, is to download it from the Internet. However great care should be taken when using the internet as viruses can easily be transferred to a computer while using the internet.

Operating System

The operating system, is a collection of systems software programs, which are used to manage the computer. These programs are automatically loaded when the computer is switched on. The most common operating system is Microsoft Windows. This operating system has developed over the past decade and is now extensively the operating system which is used on PCs. The system is very user friendly, making extensive use of the mouse and screen icons to operate the computer.

The operating system manages all the resources available to the computer, such as RAM, disk storage, keyboard, mouse, printer, CD ROM/DVD, etc. The operating system also provides support to the applications software when it wants to use any of the items just mentioned.

Some of the most common applications software would include word processors, spreadsheets, database management systems, graphics programs, accounts programs, games etc.

Files and Folders

Any data which is stored on a computer must be stored in a file and given a file name. The computer then stores that file and records the filename in a special table called a File Allocation Table (FAT). If you are using windows as the operating system then filenames can be practically anything you like to name them.

All files stored on a computers hard disk are contained in folders. Some thought should be given to how many folders you require, what they will be named and the folder structure to be used, as this will make the locating of files easy.

Data Accuracy

Computers are very efficient at processing data. The computer will process the data supplied to it in whatever way the program instructs it to do so. If the data supplied to the computer is not accurate then the computer has no way of knowing that, and it will therefore produce incorrect results, as far as the operator is concerned.

In the case of accounts, if an item is entered into the accounts program at a selling price of €12.50 instead of €125.00, then the computer will happily invoice this item at €12.50 each and will accurately calculate the cost on any number of them. The program will also calculate the amount of VAT to be charged. The program will also update all relevant accounts without any error. The error in this case is human error and therefore it is most important to ensure accuracy of data being entered into computer files, particularly in accounting programs. In most cases the computer has no way of checking the accuracy of data entered.

Security

In running a business using a computerised accounting program it is most important that the accounts stored on the computer are secure. Most accounting software packages will not allow access to the accounts without the user inputting a user code and a password. These codes should be kept secure and not left written on a piece of paper stuck to the machine. It is a good idea to change user passwords fairly frequently.

Most accounting programs also provide a means of restricting the access of users to certain parts of the program. Every user should be given access only to those sections of the program which they need access to and restricted from accessing other sections.

A major threat to computer security nowadays is the threat from computer viruses. These are easily picked up from floppy disks and from the internet and e-mail. Each computer should have an up to date virus protection program installed which will detect a virus and warn the user. There should be a definite policy on using floppy disks on a computer. If you are not sure that a disk is virus free then it should not be inserted in the disk drive.

Information stored on a computer's hard disk should be backed up (copied) onto floppy disk or tape at regular intervals. The frequency of this process should be dictated by the consequences of loosing the data. It is common practice to perform daily, weekly and monthly backups of sensitive data.

PART III

COMPUTERISED BOOKKEEPING

8. Computerised Bookkeeping

Computerised bookkeeping/accounts programs (packages) make the running of a business very simple by providing a simple method of recording all transactions which affect the business. Computerised bookkeeping will do everything which can be done using a manual system of bookkeeping, and in effect they are simply a manual system transferred to a computer. The computer saves time and money and eliminates repetition while still maintaining the integrity of the accounts. For example, the entry of a single sales invoice will update the sales daybook and will automatically update the customer's account, the debtors' control account, the sales account, the VAT account along with the profit and loss account and balance sheet. This all happens automatically provided the data is input correctly and there is no need to worry about the knock-on effects.

These notes are written in a very practical manner. Each task is set out individually and step-by-step instructions are given on how to perform that task. The tasks follow the same sequence as the manual section with the same source documents being used for both manual and computerised. This means that the manual and computerised books may be compared at all stages. It may be very helpful to compare the output from the computer program with the manual daybooks and ledgers at regular intervals as this will enhance the understanding of both systems of bookkeeping.

The disadvantage of following this sequence of tasks is that we will not be covering each section of the computer program individually, but rather jumping from one section to another in order to carry out the required task. However, the summary section will assist you in performing each task later and locating the page containing the detail on how to perform that task. The contents page will also allow you to locate the page containing the required instructions on performing any task.

There are quite a number of computerised bookkeeping (accounting) programs available and the tasks are designed to be used with any computerised program. Each task has been specifically explained using TAS Books Accounting Plus and the screens shown are from that program. However, these screens are very similar to other TAS programs and it should be very easy to work with any of the TAS Accounting/Bookkeeping programs.

If another accounting program is being used the tasks will be exactly the same and the source documents supplied are designed to be used with any program. The data to be input will be the same no matter what program is being used. However, the screens displayed by another program, for the input of this data, may appear different but there should be no difficulty in performing each task.

The tasks in this section start with the assumption that the accounting/bookkeeping program is installed on the computer and that the company J.P. Murphy Electric has been created.

Detailed instructions for installing TAS Books Accounting Plus and for creating the company J.P. Murphy Electric are contained in Part IV.

TAS Books Accounting Plus

The following are some general notes on bookkeeping and on the TAS Books Accounting Plus program, such as how to select the program on a computer, how to select the correct section, and how to move from field to field etc. Some of these notes are also applicable to other programs.

Note: In these notes the symbol **[S]** is used to indicate that you should Select the option which follows the **[S]** symbol by pointing to it with the mouse and clicking the left mouse button. For example if you were being asked to select the Sales menu the notes would read:

[S] 2 Sales   This would mean that you should point to 2 Sales on the menu bar at the top of the screen with the mouse pointer and click the left mouse button.

This symbol will be used extensively throughout this book.

Fields

All data contained in computerised accounting programs is stored in fields. Each separate field contains one piece of data. When particular data, such as a customers account code, is entered into a record, it is stored as a key field. This means that this field can be used to search for particular records, even if you do not know the full code. There are a number of key fields used by TAS Books Accounting Plus. Each key field will be recognised because it is displayed in bold print. There will be a key field at least once in every record.

NOTE: *1. One very important key is the **Tab Key** (⬅➡). Pressing this key moves the cursor from one field (box) to the next. This is the method used to enter the data in a field and move on to the next field, when inputting data into the computer.*
2. Another very useful key is the F2 function key which will display all the entries in a particular key field in which the cursor is positioned.

Some fields display a selection icon (▼) on the right-hand side of the field. When this icon is beside a field it means that you must select one of the options displayed when you click on this button. It is often possible to select the option required by typing the first letter of the option and the program then recognises this as one of the possible options and displays that option. One of the options is usually displayed and that option may be accepted by pressing the Tab key to move onto the next field.

The entry of every document in the computerised program requires at least one date to be entered. Dates are entered by typing the digits only, the slashes between the day, month and year are not typed. Dates consist of six or eight digits, i.e. two day digits, two month digits and two or four year digits (depending on the setup). Leading zeros are used where there are single figures, e.g. the sixth day would be typed as 06. Very often it is only necessary to type the two day digits and then press the tab key to move to the next field.

Function Keys

The function keys, F1 — F10, on the top row of your computer keyboard are used to perform special tasks. Some of these functions are also available as buttons, at the bottom, lefthand corner, of the screen. The functions are operated by simply pressing the appropriate function key or by pointing to the appropriate function button and clicking the left mouse button.

The functions which are available using the function keys and buttons are as follows:

Key	Button	Operation
F1		Display a help screen
F2		Selects the lookup function for key fields
F3		Clear the record which is on screen
F4		Delete the record on screen
F5	◀	Find the first record in the file
F6	▶	Find the last record in the file
F7	◀	Find the previous record to the one on screen
F8	▶	Find the next record to the one on screen
F9	▶	Find the nearest record to what has been entered in a key field
F10		Save the record on screen to file

On Screen Instructions

Each time the program requires you to enter data or perform a certain task, it will prompt you with a simple instruction. These instructions appear at the bottom of the screen. (You may have to scroll down the screen to see them, depending on your screen settings.)

Double Entry

Accounting/Bookkeeping programs use a double entry system for the entry of all amounts into the accounts system. This is a standard method used in accounting and there are many fine books written to explain the system. However, as far as you are concerned you must adopt the rule; that every entry in the system must have an amount(s) in the Debit column and an amount(s) in the Credit column. The totals of both columns must match exactly to the last cent in order for the entry to be valid. The number of entries in both columns does not matter, as long as the totals are the same. This will be explained further when we are posting to the ledgers and when entering source documents into the computer program.

Selecting the TAS Books Accounting Plus Program.

The program is started in the normal way as follows:

Shortcut

> If there is an icon on the screen for TAS Books Accounting Plus, then the program is selected by simply pointing to that icon and double clicking the left mouse button.

Task Bar (Start)

> All programs may be started by clicking the start button on the task bar. This will produce a pop-up menu, which will display the available options. As you move the mouse over the menu the various options will be highlighted. Highlight the Programs option and another menu will appear. Move the mouse pointer into the new menu and highlight the TAS Books Accounting Plus option and another menu will appear. Point to the TAS Books Accounting Plus program and click the left mouse button.

Once the program has been selected it will be loaded and will automatically display the TAS Books Accounting Plus – Multi-Company Selection window (assuming a multi-company version). This window will list the companies available on your computer.

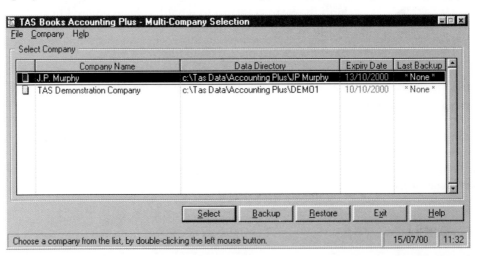

Point to the company required and click the left mouse button. Then point to the Select button and click the left mouse button again. Alternatively you may point to the company required and double click the left mouse button.

Entering the TAS Books Accounting Plus Program

Once you select the required company, the following welcome screen will be displayed:

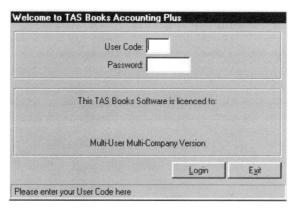

As accounting programs contain a great deal of sensitive information the program is protected by a User Code and a Password.

Type the Correct User Code (This will be given to you) and press the Tab key.

Type the Correct Password (This will be given to you) and **[S] Login** or press the Enter key.

Selecting the Correct Section

The TAS Books Accounting Plus program has a number of various sections, which are listed as menus on the menu bar at the top of the screen, as shown below:

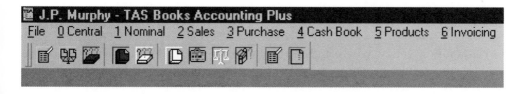

The various sections are selected by simply pointing to the required section and clicking the left mouse button. Once you select one of the sections listed above, a drop down menu will appear under the menu selected. Move the mouse down the menu and each section will be highlighted, and a second, sub menu will appear. This sub menu lists the individual options which are available from that particular menu. Move the mouse into the sub menu area and these options will be highlighted. Highlight the option required and click the left mouse button.

All options are run by selecting from three menus (or from an icon on the toolbar). For example, in order to print the sales and cash daybooks, the correct option is selected as follows:

[S] 2 Sales   (the Sales menu will appear on screen)

[S] 4 Sales Ledger Reports   (the Sales Ledger Reports menu will appear)

[S] 1 Print Sales / Cash Daybooks   (the Print Sales / Cash Daybooks screen will appear)

When this screen is displayed it will appear as shown below:

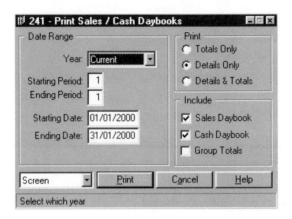

You will notice that this screen is titled **241 – Print Sales / Cash Daybooks.** The number **241** is derived from the individual numbers selected in order to select this particular option, thus producing a three digit number.

All options have a three-digit number, and as you use the program you will begin to know the three-digit number associated with particular options. Once you know the number you may find it quicker to select that option as follows:

Hold down the Alt key and type the three-digit number, *using the numbers on the top row of the keyboard.* The menus will appear as you type the numbers and the option chosen will appear as soon as you type the last digit.

Customising the Company

In a classroom situation, where each student is usually working with identical companies it is impossible to distinguish one student's company from another's. In such cases it is very useful to amend the company name to include the student's name or initials. This also helps in the identification of printouts as the company name (as amended) will appear on all printouts.

This option of amending the company name is accomplished as follows:

[S] 0 Central
[S] 1 General Company Information
[S] 1 Maintain Company Information

The program will then display the Maintain Company Information screen, and will display a message informing you that a lock has been placed on some of the company files as shown below:

[S] OK to continue.

The screen for the input of the company general information will be displayed. Use the mouse to place the cursor beside the name 'J.P. Murphy' and click the left mouse button twice, slowly (you must perform two separate clicks in order to place the cursor after the company name). Enter your name or initials, in brackets, after the company name. When you have completed this task the screen should look like the following:

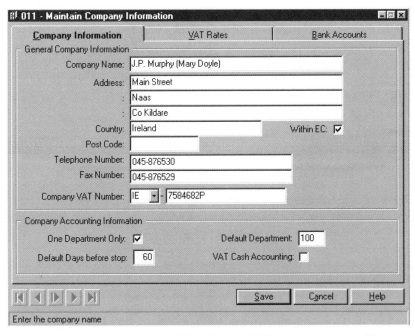

[S] Save and the company name will be changed. The new name will appear on all printouts but will not appear on the top line of the program until you logout and login to the company again.

Reports

There are a great number of reports which may be obtained from a computerised bookkeeping program. Running these reports causes the program to search the company files and assemble the required information in an understandable format. The running of any of these reports does not update the files and they can therefore be run as often as required.

The presentation of the reports is defined by the program and it is therefore only necessary to select the report required and input some simple selections for each report. Each report will provide prompts with the most likely options and generally it is only necessary to press the Tab key to accept the options offered. The prompt line at the bottom of the screen will provide instructions with what to input each time a piece of data is required.

Most reports require the input of the Starting and Ending Periods or the Starting and Ending Dates for the report. When inputting Starting and Ending periods (months) it must be remembered that period 1 is the first period of the financial year of the company. This can be any month of the year, and not necessarily January. The period numbers are counted from the first month of the financial year.

Exiting the TAS Books Accounting Plus Program.

At the end of each session you must exit the program correctly. Before attempting to exit the program, make sure all that all TAS Books windows are closed. The program is exited as follows:

[S] File   *or*   **[S]** ☒ Close Program Button

[S] Exit TAS Books

The program will then display a window asking you if you want to exit TAS Books, as shown below.

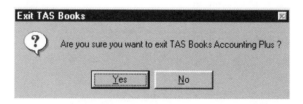

[S] **Yes** and the program will shut down.

Closing the TAS Books Accounting Plus – Multi-Company Selection window

When you selected the company which you were using, the TAS Books Accounting Plus – Multi-Company Selection window minimised itself, and is still displayed on the taskbar. This window must also be closed as follows:

[S] ⬜ TAS Books Accounting TAS Books Accounting Plus on the taskbar. (The window will reappear on screen.)

[S] The Exit Button   *or*   **[S]** ☒ The program close button

9. Sales Invoices and Credit Notes

We will begin our work on the computer in the same place as with the manual bookkeeping section. In order to begin with this first task the company J.P. Murphy Electric must already be set up on your computer and some Products, Customers and Suppliers already entered.

Details on setting up this company are contained in Part IV.

> **Task C-1**
>
> Produce an Invoice from the details of the first invoice on Source Documents page 1.

The procedure of producing an Invoice is two-fold. First, the customer and product details must be entered on a Sales Order. Secondly, the Sales order is then Printed and Posted in order to produce the Invoice and Post the details to the correct daybook and ledgers.

Enter Sales Order

This option is used to create sales invoices, quotations etc. by entering the customer details and the details of products/services to be supplied. This option is selected as follows:

[S] 6 Invoicing

[S] 1 Sales Orders

[S] 1 Enter / Change Invoices / Cr Notes

The program then presents a screen for the input of the order details.

This screen consists of three sections, Order Details, Customer Details and Payment Details, each with a selection tab at the top. The first section is used to enter the product/service details the second section is used to display the customer details and the third section is for payment details. Enter the invoice details in the Order Details section. The information to be entered is as follows:

Invoice To:	Enter the Customer Code for this invoice and then press the Tab key. (Pressing the F2 function key will display a list of customers. The full list of customers and customer codes for this company are on Source Documents page 56.)
Deliver To:	This field is for the selection of a delivery address which has been input with the customer details. Press the Tab key to skip this field and move to the next field.

Order. No: This field is used for retrieving existing orders which have *not* been printer and posted. Orders are retrieved by skipping the 'Invoice To' field and inputting an existing order number. The order will be displayed and may then be edited or deleted, provided it has not been processed, as described later. This field is skipped when entering a new order.

Date: Type the date for this order (invoice, credit note etc.).

Type: Select Invoice, Quotation, Pro-Forma Inv, Packing Slip or Credit Note by **[S]** ▼ selection icon and then selecting the option required. (Invoice will be displayed automatically so press the Tab key to accept Invoice and move to the next field.

Ref: Used for the input of customer order numbers, where they are used.

     Accept defaults for – Desc:, Disc:, Days:, VAT:, Sales Person and Market Code by pressing the Tab key to move onto the next field.

Product Code: Type the product code for each item and the details for that item will be displayed. (Pressing the F2 function key will display a list of products. The full list of products and product codes for this company are on Source Documents page 59.)

Qty: Type the number of this product to be invoiced.

     The Unit Price, Disc%, and VAT rate will be displayed for this product. Press the Tab key to accept the default values.

When you have entered the required details the screen should look like the following:

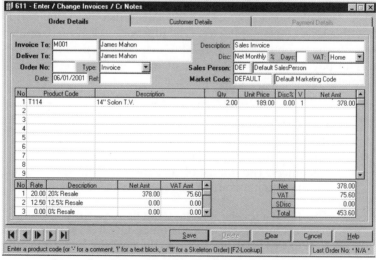

[S] Save to save this order. (You may use the F10 function key to save.)

The following window will then appear:

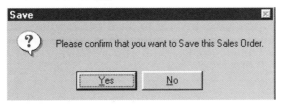

[S] **Yes** to confirm to save this Sales Order.

The program will generate an Order No which will be used in processing this order. The order number may be used to recall this order and modify or delete it before processing, as mentioned above and will be explained later.

Print and Post Sales Invoices and Credit Notes

Any sales order which has been entered as Invoice or Credit Note must be printed and posted. Printing will produce the invoice or credit note on hard copy and posting will enter the invoice in the sales daybook, the customers account in the sales ledger and the debtors control account in the nominal ledger. The procedure is as follows:

[S] 6 Invoicing

[S] 2 Print / Post

[S] 5 Print Sales Invoices / Credit Notes

The program then displays a screen for the input of some data. This screen offers a number of options which may be selected/entered, but generally it is sufficient to accept the options offered by the program. The options which may be changed are as follows:

Sort Type:	This section offers the option of printing Orders or Reprinting Invoices. Select the option required by clicking on it and ensuring that the black dot is in the circle of the option required.
Starting Order/Invoice Number:	This is the Starting Order number for orders or the Starting Invoice Number for reprinting invoices. Enter a particular number if required or accept the number offered.
Ending Order/Invoice Number:	This is the Ending Order number for orders or the Ending Invoice Number for reprinting invoices. Enter a particular number if required or accept the number offered.
Auto Post orders after Printing:	This option automatically posts the order after it has been printed. This should be ticked when printing orders.

Print Preview	The screen offers the option of a print preview. This may be selected by clicking its check box to place a tick in the box.

All the other options should be correct but you may change any of the other options offered, if necessary.

When the options are selected/entered the screen should look like the following:

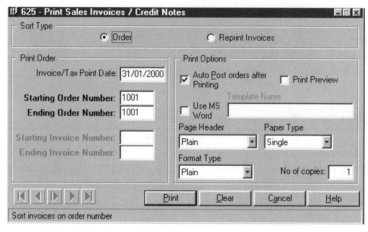

[S] Print, and the Invoice(s) or Credit Note(s) will be printed.

When the Invoice/Credit Note has been sent to the printer, and the Auto post option has been ticked, the program will display the posting screen and display a message stating that the invoice(s)/Credit Note(s) has/have been posted.

[S] OK and the posting will be complete.

If your computer is not connected to a printer then an error message, similar to that shown below, may appear on screen.

If you **[S] Cancel** the posting will be completed but the invoice/credit note will not be printed.

Task C-2

Produce Invoices from the details of the remaining invoices on Source Documents page 1.

Task C-3

Produce a Credit Note from the details of the Credit Note on Source Documents page 1.

The production of a credit note is exactly the same as an invoice with the exception that you select Credit Note when entering the Sales Order instead of an Invoice.

NOTE: *When you print and post a Credit Note it will credited to the customers account in the sales ledger but will not be allocated against the invoice. It is therefore necessary to alloate the credit note as will be described later.*

Task C-4   (Optional)

Display Sales Order number 1001 on Screen

Sales Order Enquiry

This option allows the details of any sales order to be displayed on screen and/or on hard copy.

This option is selected as follows:

[S] 6 Invoicing

[S] 1 Sales Orders

[S] 2 Sales Order Enquiry

The program then displays a screen for the input of the Customer Code or the Order Number. The data to be input is as follows:

Customer Code:	Type a customer code if you know the customer code for the sales order required. Press the Tab key to skip this field.
Sales Order Number:	Enter the sales order number. (If you do not know the sales order number you may use the F2 function key to obtain a list of sales orders. If you have entered a customer code then the sales orders for that customer only will be dis played when you press the F2 key.)
Include Address:	Tick this box, by pointing to it and clicking the left mouse button, if you wish to have the customer's address included in the output.
Screen:	This field indicates that the enquiry is being sent to the screen.

When the data is entered the screen should look like the following:

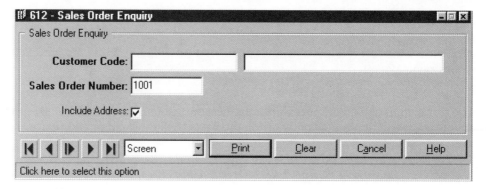

[S] **Print** to output the details to the screen.

[S] **Print** on the screen output the produce a hard copy of the enquiry.

Any sales order may be recalled at any time and changes made to it, provided it has not been printed and posted. If the sales order has been printed and posted then no alterations may be made.

Task C-5   (Optional)

Recall Sales Order number 1002.

Recalling a Sales Order

A sales order may be recalled in order to change the details on the order or to convert from one order type to another, e.g. to convert a Quotation into an actual Invoice. The order may be recalled as follows:

 [S] 6 Invoicing

 [S] 1 Sales Orders

 [S] 1 Enter / Change Invoices / Cr Notes

The Enter / Change Invoices / Cr Notes screen will be displayed. This is the same screen which was used to enter the order.

Press the Tab Key to move directly to the **Order No** field.

Type the Sales Order number required and then press the Tab key.

(Remember you may use the F2 function key to display a list of orders.)

The sales order will be displayed. It may be edited or deleted, provided it has not been processed.

If the order has been processed then the following window will be displayed:

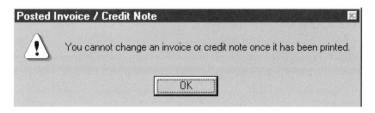

[S] **OK** and the sales order will be displayed with the following message displayed in the middle of the sales order.

> This Order has been printed and posted.
>
> Invoice Number: 1002 Date: 31/01/2000

10. Sales Ledger

The Sales Ledger is used to store all the information relating to customers. All invoices, credit notes and receipts are recorded in the sales ledger. When an invoice or credit notes is created using the invoicing section it is automatically recorded in the sales ledger.

Allocate Customer (Sales) Credit Notes

Once a payment has been received, from a customer (debtor) it must be entered and allocated (matched) to the particular invoice to which it relates.

When a credit note has been entered it must also be allocated against the relevant invoice. For this purpose the credit note is treated as a part payment against the invoice, and therefore it must be allocated in the same way as a Receipt in the Sales Ledger.

> **Task C-6**
>
> Allocate the Credit Note on Source Documents page 1 issued to New Age Contractors

Customer Receipts and Sales Credit Notes are allocated as follows:

- **[S] 2 Sales**
- **[S] 5 Receipts**
- **[S] 1 Enter / Allocate Sales Ledger Receipts**

The program will then display the Enter / Allocate Sales Ledger Receipts screen. This screen has three sections for the input of information, as follows:

Bank and Posting Details	
Bank:	This is the bank account into which the receipt will be entered.
	In the case of Receipts select '1 – Current Bank A/C', by **[S] ▼** in the Bank field and selecting '1 - Current Bank A/C' or simply press the number 1 for this account.
	In the case of a credit notes, or the allocation of a receipt which has been entered but has not been allocated, there will be no bank account involved so accept '0 - None [Existing Receipt]' by pressing the Tab key to move directly to Code.
Date:	The Sales Ledger date will be displayed. Press the Tab key to accept this date for receipts.
Code:	Enter the code for this customer.
	In the case of a credit note or an unallocated receipt the remaining details will be entered automatically. A list of all unallocated receipts and credit notes will be displayed.
Owed:	The outstanding balance for this customer will be displayed automatically.

Receipt Details

Slip Ref: Enter the lodgement slip number for receipts.

Reconciled: Indicates whether the lodgement is reconciled or not.

Cheque No: Enter the number of the cheque received for receipts or the word Cash for cash sales. (Remember that cash sales must be entered here immediately after producing the invoice as the money is received immediately.)

Cheque Date: Enter the lodgement date for receipts.

Descriptions: SL Receipt will be displayed by pressing the Tab key. Sales Credit Note will be displayed automatically when allocating credit notes. Enter the word Cash when entering and allocating cash sales.

Amount: Enter the amount of the receipt. The amount of a credit note will be displayed automatically.

Unalloc: The amount still unallocated will be displayed. If the receipt is being allocated against a number of invoices then this amount will decrease as allocations are made. The allocation is complete when this figure is zero.

Cash / Credit for Allocation

Post No: The posting number of the payment or credit note is displayed.

Type: The journal type is displayed.

Inv/Rcpt No: The invoice, credit note number is displayed.

Inv/Rcpt Date: The invoice, cheque or credit note date is displayed.

Description: The description of the posting is displayed.

Amount: The amount of receipt or credit note is displayed.

Rem Bal/Unall: The amount still due or unallocated is displayed.

S: Indicates the status of the posting. The letter A indicates allocated.

Once you enter the Code the outstanding Credit Note(s), and/or any unallocated receipts will be displayed on the screen as shown below:

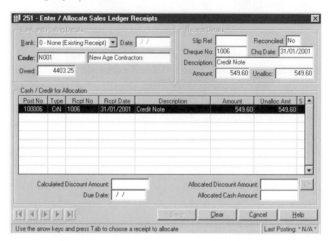

Select the credit note to be allocated using the arrow keys to move up and down the list, if there is more than one, until the required credit note is highlighted. Press the Tab key when the correct credit note is highlighted and the Receipt Details section will automatically be filled in.

The following window will then be displayed:

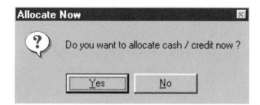

[S] Yes

The bottom half of the screen will then change to display a list of the outstanding invoices for this customer. Use the arrow keys to select the invoice to which the payment/credit note relates, if there is more than one invoice.

Press the Tab key and the 'Allocate Discount Amount' field will display 0.00. If there is a discount on this invoice it would be entered here.

Press the Tab key twice more to skip the 'Split discount into adjustment button' (<->) and the 'Allocate Cash Amount' field will display the amount to be allocated.

Press the Tab key once more to accept the amount of the allocation or enter the amount to be allocated and then press the Tab key. If the receipt/credit note is not for the full amount of the invoice then a window will appear on screen, informing you that this invoice is only part paid, as shown below:

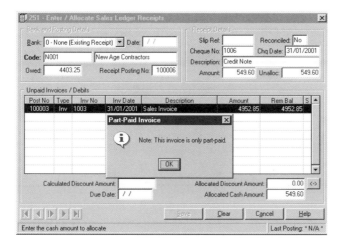

[S] OK and the invoice amount will be reduced by the amount of the payment/credit note. The letter A will appear in the S (Status) column to indicate that this receipt or credit note has been allocated.

The following window will then appear.

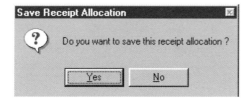

[S] Yes and the allocation is complete.

Enter and Allocate Customer Receipts

The procedure for performing this task is very similar to allocating a credit note as described above.

Task C-7

Enter and Allocate the cheque received from James Mahon on Source Documents page 8.

Monies received from customers are entered and allocated as follow:

[S] 2 Sales

[S] 5 Receipts

[S] 1 Enter / Allocate Sales Ledger Receipts

The program will then display the 'Enter / Allocate Sales Ledger Receipts' screen as shown above for allocating credit notes.

In this case the Bank Current A/C (usually Bank Account No 1) must be selected as the cheque is lodged to the bank. The details of the receipt must be entered as described above.

When the receipt details have been entered the following window will be displayed:

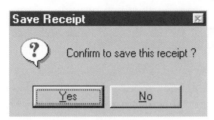

[S] **Yes** and the following window will be displayed:

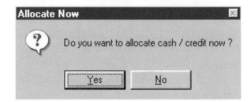

[S] **Yes** and the invoices with outstanding balances will be displayed.

Complete the allocation as described above for allocating a credit note.

Task C-8

Enter and Allocate the cash received for the cash sale invoice.

(The amount of the receipt was €49.95 and the lodgement number was 102)

Every time an invoice is processed for a cash sale the money which is received at the time of sale must be entered and allocated in the same way as a cheque received from a customer. In the case of cash sales the word Cash would normally be written in the cheque number field and the word Cash would be entered in the Description field, instead of SL Receipt

Task C-9

Enter and Allocate the remaining cheques received on Source Documents pages 8–9.

Sales and Cash Daybooks

There are a great number of reports available from the computer program. Some of these reports are very similar to the daybooks and ledgers as produced manually. There are also a number of extra reports which provide information not readily available from the manual system.

> ### Task C-10
>
> (a)   Produce a Sales Daybook report and compare this with your sales/sales returns daybook produced manually for January.
>
> (b)   Produce a Debtors (Customers) Receipts report and compare this with your cash receipts (bank lodgement) book produced manually for January.

The sales daybook report will produce a list of sales invoices and credit notes similar to the sales daybook produced manually. The cash daybook report, from the sales ledger will produce a list of monies received from customers. This report is similar to the Cash Receipts (Bank Lodgement) Book produced manually, but will only contain receipts from customers and will not include any monies entered through the cash book.

The sales daybook and the customer receipts report are produced as follows:

[S] 2 **Sales**

[S] 4 **Sales Ledger Reports**

[S] 1 **Print Sales / Cash Daybooks**

This report is actually two reports in one. It will produce a sales daybook and/or a cash (customers) receipts daybook.

When this option is selected the following screen will be displayed:

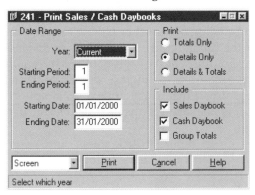

In this case the options offered are correct. The periods and dates for the report are correct with the options to print a sales daybook and a cash daybook ticked, therefore both reports will be produced. If you only needed one report then it is a simple matter of removing the tick from the report which is not required.

[S] Print and the both reports will appear on screen, with one report in front of the other. The second report may be displayed by pointing to the grey band beside the report name and clicking the left mouse button.

A hard copy of a report is produced by simply **[S] Print** on the screen report.

NOTE: *You may have to scroll down and scroll right to see the full report on screen, depending on your screen size and resolution.*

Task C-11 (Optional)

Produce a report showing all the transactions for New Age Contractors

---

Customer Account Enquiry

This option is used to view the transactions contained in one particular customer's account. The option is selected as follows:

[S] 2 Sales

[S] 1 Customers

[S] 2 Customer Account Enquiry

The program then displays the screen used to enter new customers (we will be entering new customers later). Enter the customer code and press the Tab key. (If you do not know the full code, then entering the first part and pressing the F9 function key or the |▶ button, at the bottom of the screen, will display the nearest customer code. Pressing the F2 key will display the full list of customers. The list of customers for this company is contained on Source Documents page 56.)

The program automatically defaults to displaying the Open Items only (i.e. items that have not been cleared by being allocated or having a receipt and/or a credit note allocated against them for the full amount). If you wish to display all items then the field beside the function key buttons, at the bottom of the screen, must be changed to display 'All Items'. This is accomplished by **[S]** ▼ beside the window, displaying 'Open Items'. A short drop down menu will appear, so simply click on 'All Items'. The start date for the report is displayed in the next field. This date may be changed when All Items are selected.

Enter the code, change 'Open Items' to 'All Items' and enter the start date as 01/01/##. The screen should then look like the following:

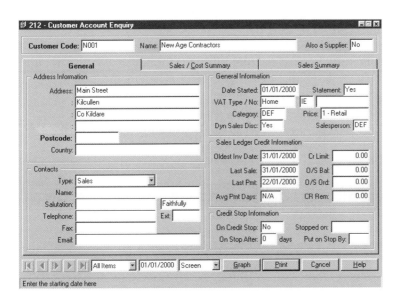

The field beside the date indicates that the report will be sent to the screen.

[S] Print and the report will be displayed, on the screen.

When the report is displayed on the screen you may send it to the printer by simply clicking the Print button at the bottom of the report. Click the Cancel button if you do not want to send it to the printer. This will close the window and return you to the previous window, where you may look at another customer's account or click the Cancel button to close the window.

11. Purchase Ledger

The Purchase Ledger is used to store all the information relating to suppliers. All invoices, credit notes and payments are recorded in the purchase ledger. This includes invoices (bills) for telephone and electricity. When an invoice or credit note is received it must first be entered into the purchase ledger.

Purchase Invoices

Every time a credit purchase is made, an invoice will be received by our company from the supplier. The data contained on this invoice must be entered into the computer accounts.

Task C-12

Enter the details contained on the Purchase Invoice on Source Documents page 10 into the Purchase Ledger.

The procedure for entering purchase invoices into the Purchase Ledger is as follows:

[S] 3 Purchase

[S] 2 Enter / Change Journals

[S] 1 Enter / Change Supplier Invoices / Credit Journals

The program will then display the 'Enter / Change Supplier Invoices / Credit Journals' screen.

There are three distinct sections to this screen for the input of information. The program will prompt you at the bottom of the screen with instructions. Remember to use the Tab key to move to the next field.

The information which must be entered is as follows:

Posting Details

Department: This is the department number. Always 100 in the case of single department businesses, in which case the 100 will automatically be displayed.

Posting No: This is a unique posting number issued by the program to each individual entry. Therefore it is left blank by the operator when inputting an invoice or credit note. Any entry may be altered by recalling this posting number. (The posting number for invoices or credit notes already entered may be obtained from the Purchase / Cash Daybooks. The procedure for obtaining this report is described later.)

Date: The Purchase ledger date will be displayed here. (This should be the last day of the **present** month. Do not change this date unless you are making a posting into a different month).

Source: This is the source for this entry. The letters PL are displayed, indicating the   Purchase Ledger.

Type: This is the type of entry. Accept PL Invoice.

Tip: *You may skip through this section by simply pressing the Tab key twice.*

Invoice Details

Code: Enter the code for this supplier (creditor) and then press the Tab key. (Pressing the F2 function key will display a list of suppliers. The full list of suppliers and supplier codes for this company are on Source Documents page 57.)

Name: The name of the Supplier will be displayed automatically once the code is entered.

Ref No: Enter the invoice number as displayed on the invoice.

Date: Enter the invoice date as displayed on the invoice.

Desc: This is the description for this entry and Purchase Invoice will be displayed automatically once you press the Tab key.

Net: This is the net amount as indicated on the invoice.

VAT: This is the VAT code, followed by the amount as indicated on the invoice. The VAT amount will be calculated automatically, except in the case of Multi VAT (M) code. (see below)
(Pressing the F2 key will display the list of VAT codes.)

Total: This is the total of Net plus VAT and will be calculated automatically.

Note: *If there is only one VAT rate on the invoice you may skip the Net field by pressing the Tab key, enter the VAT code and skip the VAT amount and then enter the total from the invoice in the Total field. The program will calculate and display the Net and VAT amounts automatically, but you should check that they correspond to the invoice or credit note.*

Rem Bal: This is the amount of the outstanding balance on this invoice and will be equal to the total.

Disc: This is the amount of discount on this entry. We will leave it blank, by pressing the Tab key.

Nominal Ledger Details

The bottom half of the screen is for the Nominal Ledger distribution. This is where we perform the nominal ledger double entry for this transaction. The total of the Debit column must equal the total of the Credit column for a valid entry. If the totals are not equal then the program will indicate the difference in the 'Still to Post' field.

Line 1 will be the Purchase Ledger Control account and will be a credit for   the total of the invoice.

Line 2 will be the VAT payable account and will debit the VAT amount.

The next line will allow you to debit the Expense or Asset account with the value of the goods on the invoice. If you have previously made an entry for this supplier then the account will automatically appear and you will simply have to enter the correct amount in the debit column. Otherwise you will have to enter the correct Nominal Account Number, under Account. Enter 2000 for the Purchase Account, press the tab key and then enter the correct value in the debit column. (Pressing the F2 function key will display a list of nominal accounts. The full list of nominal accounts for this company are on Source Documents page 58.)

VAT: The VAT will automatically be distributed to the correct code except in the case of multi VAT entries. In the case of multi VAT entries the program will automatically display a window for the distribution of VAT. Enter the amounts, *as indicated on the invoice*, to the correct codes. Press the Tab key after each entry. When an acceptable entry has been entered the OK button will become active and you may click on it to continue to the next section. If the OK button does not become active then the entries are not complete or the entries in the VAT section do not match the entries in the previous section. We will not have any multi VAT rate purchases.

When you have entered the required details the screen should look like the following:

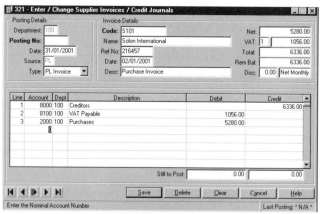

[S] **Save** and the following window will be displayed:

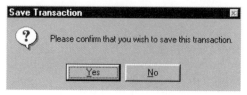

[S] **Yes** and the transaction will be saved.

Task C-13

Enter the details contained on the Purchase Invoices on Source Documents pages 11–12 into the Purchase Ledger.

Task C-14

Enter the details contained on the Purchase Credit Note on Source Documents page 13 into the Purchase Ledger.

Purchase Credit Notes

Credit notes which are received from suppliers must also be entered into the purchase ledger and allocated against the relevant invoice. Purchase credit notes are entered in the Purchase Ledger as follows:

[S] 3 **Purchase Ledger**

[S] 2 **Enter / Change Journals**

[S] 2 **Enter / Change Supplier Credit Notes / Debit Journals**

The screen display is the same as the Purchase invoice screen. The entries made in the various sections are exactly the same as for the Purchase invoice. VAT distribution should be input as with the invoice. In the case of a Purchase Credit Note the Creditors Control account is debited with the amount of the credit note and the VAT and Purchase accounts are credited with the respective amounts.

NOTE: *Remember that once you enter the credit note you must allocate it, that is match the credit note to the relevant invoice in order to reduce the invoice by the amount of the credit note. The credit note is treated as a part payment against the invoice, and therefore it must be entered as a Payment into the Purchase Ledger.*

Allocate Purchase Ledger Credit Notes

When a credit note has been entered it must also be allocated against the relevant invoice. For this purpose the credit note is treated as a part payment against the invoice, and therefore it must be allocated in the same way as a Payment in the Purchase Ledger.

Task C-15

Allocate the Credit Note on Source Documents page 13 received from Solon International.

Supplier Payments and Purchase Credit Notes are allocated as follows:

[S] 3 Purchase

[S] 5 Payments on Account

[S] 1 Enter / Allocate Purchase Ledger Payments

The program will then display the 'Enter / Allocate Purchase Ledger Payments' screen.

This screen has three sections for the input of information, as follows:

Bank and Posting Details

Bank:
This is the bank account into which the payment will be entered. In the case of Payments select '1 Current Bank A/C', by **[S]** ▼ in the Bank field and selecting '1 - Current Bank A/C' or simply press the number 1 for this account.

In the case of a credit notes, or the allocation of a payment which has not been allocated, there will be no bank account involved so accept '0 - None [Existing Payment]' by pressing the Tab key to move directly to Code.

Date:
The Purchase Ledger date will be displayed. Press the Tab key to accept for payments.

Code:
Enter the code for this Supplier.

In the case of a credit note or an unallocated payment the remaining details will be entered automatically. A list of all unallocated payments and credit notes will be displayed

Owed:
The outstanding balance for this Supplier will be displayed automatically.

Payment Details

Recon Ref:
The cheque number, for payments, will appear when the cheque number is entered in the field below.

Reconciled:
Indicates whether a payment is reconciled or not.

Cheque No:
Enter the cheque number for payments. The credit note number will appear when allocating credit notes.

Cheque Date:
Enter the date on the cheque or remittance advice in the case of payments. The credit note date will be displayed for allocating credit notes.

Descriptions:
PL Payment will be displayed by pressing the Tab key. Credit Note will be displayed for allocating credit notes.

Amount:
Enter the amount of the payment. In the case of a credit note allocation the credit note amount will be displayed.

Unalloc:
This field indicates the amount still unallocated.

Payment Allocation	
Post No:	The posting number of the payment or credit note.
Type:	The journal type.
Inv/Pmt No:	Invoice, credit note number.
Inv/Pmt Date:	Invoice, cheque or credit note date.
Description:	Description of the posting.
Amount:	Amount of payment or credit note.
Rem Bal/Unalloc:	The amount still due or unallocated.
S:	Indicates the status of the posting.

Once you enter the Code the outstanding Credit Note(s), and/or any unallocated payments will be displayed on the screen as shown below:

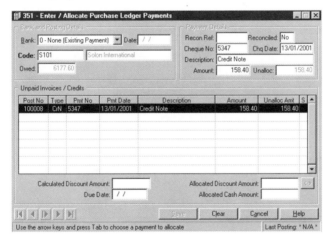

Select the credit note to be allocated using the arrow keys to move up and down the list, if there is more than one, until the required credit note is highlighted. Press the Tab key when the correct credit note is highlighted and the Payment Details section will automatically be filled in.

The following window will then be displayed:

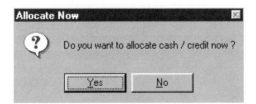

[S] Yes

The bottom half of the screen will then change to display a list of the outstanding invoices for this supplier. Use the arrow keys to select the invoice to which the payment/credit note relates, if there is more than one invoice.

Press the Tab key and the 'Allocate Discount Amount' field will display 0.00. If there is a discount on this invoice it would be entered here.

Press the Tab key twice more to skip the 'Split discount into adjustment button ' (<->) and the 'Allocate Cash Amount' field will display the amount to be allocated.

Press the Tab key once more to accept the amount of the allocation or enter the amount to be allocated and then press the Tab key. If the receipt/credit note is not for the full amount of the invoice then a window will appear on screen, informing you that this invoice is only part paid, as shown below:

[S] OK and the invoice amount will be reduced by the amount of the payment/credit note. The letter A will appear in the S (Status) column to indicate that this invoice/credit note has been allocated.

The following window will then appear.

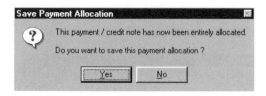

[S] Yes and the allocation is complete.

Enter and Allocate Supplier Payments

Once a payment has been made to a Supplier (creditor) it must be entered and allocated against the particular invoice to which it relates.

> **Task C-16**
>
> Enter and Allocate the Remittance Advice for Philem Ireland on Source Documents page 14.

Payments to suppliers are usually accompanied with a remittance advice which details the payment being made. In our case payments to suppliers are entered and allocated as follows:

[S] 3 Purchase

[S] 5 Payments on Account

[S] 1 Enter / Allocate Purchase Ledger Payments

The program will then display the Enter / Allocate Purchase Ledger Payments screen as shown above for allocating credit notes.

In this case the Bank Current A/C (usually Bank Account No 1) must be selected as the cheque is drawn on the bank. The details of the payment must be entered as described above.

When the payment details have been entered the following window will be displayed:

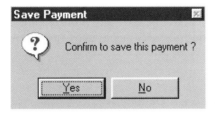

[S] Yes and the following window will be displayed:

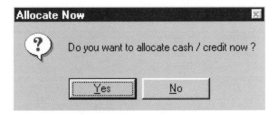

[S] Yes and the invoices with outstanding balances will be displayed.

Complete the allocation as described above for allocating a credit note.

Task C-17

Enter and Allocate the Remittance Advice for Solon International on Source Documents page 15.

Purchase and Cash Daybooks

There are a great number of reports available from the computer program. The reports which are available for sales are also available for purchases. Some of these reports are very similar to the daybooks and ledgers as produced manually. There are also a number of extra reports which provide information not readily available from the manual system.

Task C-18

(a)   Produce a Purchase Daybook report and compare this with your purchases/purchases returns daybook produced manually for January

(b)   Produce a Creditors (Supplier) Payments report and compare this with your cash (bank) payments book produced manually for January

The purchase daybook report will produce a list of purchase invoices and credit notes similar to the purchases daybook produced manually. The cash daybook report, from the purchase ledger, will produce a list of monies paid to suppliers. This report is similar to the Cash (Bank) Payments Book produced manually, but will only contain payments to suppliers and will not include any monies entered through the cash book.

The purchase daybook and the creditor payments report are produced as follows:

[S] 3 Purchase

[S] 4 Purchase Ledger Reports

[S] 1 Print Purchase / Cash Daybooks

This report is actually two reports in one. It will produce a purchase daybook and/or a cash (bank) payments book.

When this option is selected the following screen will be displayed:

In this case the options offered are correct, with the options to print a purchase day-book and a cash daybook ticked, therefore both reports will be produced. If you only needed one report then it is a simple matter of removing the tick from the report which is not required.

[S] Print and the both reports will appear on screen, with one report in front of the other. The second report may be displayed by pointing to the grey band beside the report name and clicking the left mouse button.

A hard copy of a report is produced by simply **[S] Print** on the screen report.

 NOTE: *You may have to scroll down and scroll right to see the full report on screen, depending on your screen size and resolution.*

Task C-19   (Optional)

Produce a report showing all the transactions for Solon International

---

Supplier Account Enquiry

This option is used to view the transactions contained in one particular supplier's account. The option is selected as follows:

[S] 3 Purchase

[S] 1 Suppliers

[S] 2 Supplier Account Enquiry

The program then displays the screen used to enter new suppliers (we will be performing this task later). Enter the supplier code and press the Tab key. (If you do not know the full code, then entering the first part and pressing the F9 function key or the |▶ button, at the bottom of the screen, will display the nearest supplier code. Pressing the F2 key will display the full list of suppliers). (The list of suppliers for this company is contained on Source Documents page 57.)

The program automatically defaults to displaying the Open Items only (i.e. items that have not been cleared by being allocated or having a receipt and/or a credit note allocated against them for the full amount). If you wish to display all items then the field beside the function key buttons, at the bottom of the screen, must be changed to display 'All Items'. This is accomplished by **[S] ▼** , beside the window displaying 'Open Items'. A short drop down menu will appear, so simply click on 'All Items'. The start date for the report is displayed in the next field. This date may be changed when 'All Items' are selected.

Enter the code, change 'Open Items' to 'All Items' and enter the start date as 01/01/##. The screen should then look like the following:

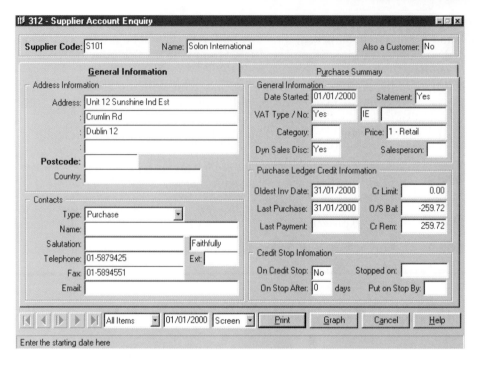

The field beside the date indicates that the report will be sent to the screen.

[S] **Print** and the report will be displayed, on the screen.

When the report is displayed on the screen you may send it to the printer by simply clicking the Print button at the bottom of the report. Click the Cancel button if you do not want to send it to the printer. This will close the window and return you to the previous window, where you may look at another supplier's account or click the Cancel button to close the window.

12. Cash Book

The payment of Salaries, Rent, VAT, PAYE/PRSI, Petty Cash purchases, etc. are recorded in the Cash Book. The monies paid out are credited to the Bank Current A/C or the Petty Cash account. The purchase of some goods for which you do not wish to set up an account in the purchase ledger, but wish to pay for by cheque, may also be entered in the cash book, credited to the Bank Current A/C and debited to the correct expense or asset account in the Nominal Ledger.

The computer Cash Book contains the equivalent of the Cash Receipts (Bank Lodgement) Book and the Cash (Bank) Payments Book on the manual system. However the receipts from customers and the payments to suppliers are recorded in the respective ledgers. The program updates the cash book automatically with the details of the receipt or payment in the Sales or Purchases Ledger.

Payments from Bank Current A/C

The entry of purchases which are not recorded in the purchase ledger and the payment of non purchase payments such as Salaries, Rent, VAT, etc. are recorded in the cash book.

> **Task C-20**
>
> A direct debit of €325.00 was made for Rent on 30/01/##. Enter this payment into the cash book.

This payment is entered as follows:

[S] 4 Cash Book

[S] 2 Enter / Change Journals

[S] 2 Enter / Change Cash Payments / Purchases

The program then presents the 'Enter / Change Cash Payments / Purchases' screen. This screen has three sections for the input of data, as follows:

Bank Account and Posting Details

Bank No: This will be the Bank Account number. Select '1 – Bank Current A/C' for cheque, Direct Debit or Standing Order payments. Select '2 – Petty Cash' for petty cash purchases.

Posting No: This is a unique posting number issued by the program to each individual entry. (Leave this blank unless recalling a posting.) Any entry may be altered by recalling this posting number. (The posting number for payments already entered may be obtained from the Cash Book Payments / Receipts report. The procedure for obtaining this report is described later).

Date: Enter the date for this transaction.

Type: Home Purchase will be displayed but you may select from the list by
          [S] ▼ and selecting from the list. In the case of Rent, salaries etc.
          which have no VAT associated with then, select **Non-VAT Jnl.**

Chq/Ref: This will be the cheque number, DD or SO in the case of Current A/C
          payments or the voucher number in the case of petty cash payments

Desc: Type a description for this payment, e.g. Salaries, Rent Payment, etc.
          In the case of petty cash enter the item(s) purchased.

Amounts

Net Amt: This is the net amount of this payment.

VAT Amt: This is the VAT code, followed by the amount of VAT on the payment.
          The VAT amount will be calculated automatically, except in the case of
          Multi VAT (**M**) code.
          (Pressing the F2 key will display the list of VAT codes.)

Total Amt: This is the total of Net plus VAT and will be calculated automatically.

          *Note: If there is only one VAT rate on the payment you may skip the
          Net field by pressing the Tab key, enter the VAT code and skip the VAT
          amount and then enter the total from the payment in the Total field. The
          program will calculate and display the Net and VAT amounts automatically.*

Nominal Ledger Details

          The bottom half of the screen is for the Nominal Ledger distribution.
          This is where we perform the nominal ledger double entry for this
          transaction. The total of the Debit column must equal the total of the
          Credit column for a valid entry. If the totals are not equal then the
          program will indicate the difference in the 'Still to Post' field.

          Line 1 will be the Bank Current A/C and will be a credit for the total
          of the payment.

          Line 2 will be the VAT payable account, *if there is VAT on the payment,*
          and will debit the VAT amount.

          The next line will allow you to debit the Expense or Asset account(s)
          with the value of the payment. Enter the correct Nominal Account
          Number, under *Account* for the account to be debited and then enter
          the correct value in the debit column. (Pressing the F2 function key
          will display a list of nominal accounts). (The full list of nominal
          accounts for this company are on Source Documents page 58.)

When you have entered all the details the screen should look like the following:

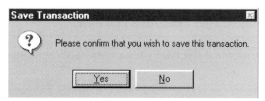

Once the double entry is correct **[S] Save** and the following window will be displayed:

[S] **Yes** and the transaction will be saved.

Petty Cash Purchases

Small items which are purchased from time to time are normally not entered in the purchase ledger and paid for by cheque. Instead, a certain amount of cash is withdrawn from the Bank Current A/C, at regular intervals, and kept as petty cash. This is then used to purchase small items. Each time a purchase is made using this cash a voucher is completed, and in some cases must be authorised. The entry of these purchases is recorded in a special bank account, called 'Petty Cash' in the Cash Book.

The entry of petty cash vouchers is the same as for payments from the current bank account, with the exception that the '2 – Petty Cash' account is selected instead of '1 – Current Bank A/C' as described above.

Task C-21

Enter the petty cash vouchers on Source Documents pages 16–18 into the Cash Book.

Restore Petty Cash Imprest

The first task to be performed at the end of each month (or some other regular interval) is to calculate the amount which was spent from petty cash and to restore the imprest to the correct amount. The company decides how much money should be in petty cash at the start of each month. This amount is called the imprest and therefore it must be restored at the end of each month before moving on to the next months transactions.

> **Task C-22**
>
> On the 31/01/## cheque number 200103 was cashed to restore the petty cash imprest. Calculate the amount of this cheque and enter it into Cash Book.

This payment is very similar to any Cash Book Payment but since the money is being paid into another bank account (petty cash) there is a slight difference, so this entry is explained separately. Restoring the petty cash imprest is accomplished as follows:

[S] 4 Cash Book

[S] 2 Enter / Change Journals

[S] 2 Enter / Change Cash Payments / Purchases

The program then presents the 'Enter / Change Cash Payments / Purchases' screen, as explained above.

In the first section of this screen, instead of accepting 'Home Purch' **[S]** ▼ in the Type field and select Inter-Bank. Once you enter the net amount the program will display the following screen:

[S] 2 – Petty Cash and **[S] OK**

When you have completed these steps the screen should look like the following with the Save Transaction window displayed:

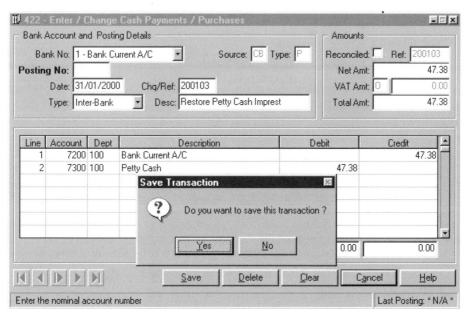

[S] **Yes** and the transaction is completed.

Cash Receipts (including Start Up Capital Investment)

Any monies received by the company which are not from customers must be lodged to the bank and recorded in the company books. When a company sets up business and prepares to start trading it invariably needs capital. This capital investment must be recorded in the company accounts and is usually the first entry in the books.

In the manual system this entry of capital investment was recorded in the General Journal. In the computerised bookkeeping system this entry may also be recorded in the general journal as described later but it is more common and correct to record the entry in the Cash Book. The entry will include the nominal accounts used in the entry and the program will automatically update the nominal ledger.

Task C-23

J.P. Murphy commenced business on 01/01/## with a capital investment of €15000.00. €14900.00 of this was deposited in their current bank account and €100.00 was placed in petty cash. Record these entries in the appropriate accounts.

Cash Book - Cash Receipts Method

Cash received, which is not as a result of issuing a Sales Invoice is normally entered into the cash book. The entry of Capital Investment is normally recorded as a cash receipt in the Bank Current A/C and a cash receipt in the Petty Cash account. The procedure for entering Cash Receipts into the Cash Book is as follows:

[S] 4 Cash Book

[S] 2 Enter / Change Journals

[S] 1 Enter / Change Cash Receipts / Sales

The program then presents the 'Enter / Change Cash Receipts / Sales' screen which is very similar to the cash payments screen. This screen has three sections for the input of data as follows:

Bank Account and Posting Details

Bank No: This will be the Bank Account number. Select '1 – Bank Current A/C' for the money lodged to the bank. Select '2 – Petty Cash' for the petty cash amount.

Posting No: This is a unique posting number issued by the program to each individual entry. Any entry may be altered by recalling this posting number.

Date: Enter the date for this transaction.

Type: Home Receipt will be displayed but you may select from list by **[S]** ▼ and selecting from the list. In the case Capital investment, which have no VAT associated with it, select **Non-VAT Jnl**.

Slip No: This will be the Lodgement Slip Number. Enter 100 for the lodgement of the capital to the Bank Current A/C. Leave blank for the Petty Cash entry.

Desc: Type a description for this receipt. e.g. 'Startup Capital Investment' in this case.

Amounts

Net Amt: This is the net amount of this receipt.

VAT Amt: This is the VAT code, followed by the amount of VAT on the payment. Since this is a non-VAT Jnl. the program will automatically skip the VAT.

Total Amt: This is the total of Net plus VAT and will be calculated automatically.

Nominal Ledger Details

The bottom half of the screen is for the Nominal Ledger distribution. This is where we perform the nominal ledger double entry for this transaction. The total of the Debit column must equal the total of the Credit column for a valid entry. If the totals are not equal then the program will indicate the difference in the 'Still to Post' field.

Line 1 will be the Bank account (either current a/c or petty cash) and will be a Debit for the total of the receipt.

Line 2 will allow you to credit the Income, or liability or Owner Equity account(s) with the net value of this receipt. Enter the correct Nominal Account Number, under Account for the account to be credited and then enter the correct value in the credit column.

(In this case 9000 for the Capital account.)

Once the data has been entered the screen should look like the following:

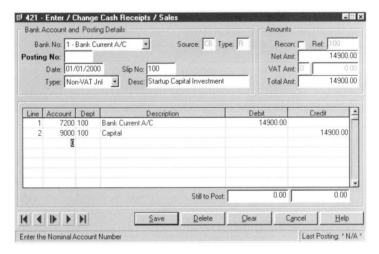

[S] Save and the following screen will be displayed:

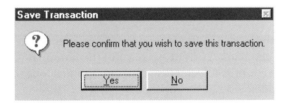

[S] Save and the Cash Receipt entry is complete.

It is now necessary to enter the receipt of the €100.00 into the Petty Cash account. The process is exactly the same as the above but this time select '2 – Petty Cash' as the Bank No. The details for the entry will be the same except that the amount will be €100.00.

General Journal Method

The entry of the Capital Investment may also be recorded through the General Journal, however, as already stated above this is not the normal method used in computerised bookkeeping, and it is only being explaining here as an entry in the General Journal and it is the method used in manual bookkeeping.

There are no source documents used in the recording of this entry. The information is contained in the task and will require three rows in the general journal.

Entries are made in the General Journal as follows:

[S] 1 General Journal

[S] 2 Enter / Change Journals

[S] 1 Enter / Change General Journals

The program then presents the 'Enter / Change General Journal' screen which has two sections for the input of data as follows:

The data to be entered is as follows:

Posting Details

Date: Enter the date of the transaction.

Description: Enter a short description for this posting.

Source: Enter the source used to make this entry. In this case there is no source document so enter **STARTUP**.

Nominal Ledger Details

Account: Enter the nominal account number.

Debit: Enter the debit amount for this entry if appropriate.

Credit: Enter the credit amount for this entry if appropriate.

The following are the three entries which are made:

1. The first entry is the record of the money lodged to the current account. This entry will be posted to the Bank Current Account in the Nominal (General) Ledger. Since the Bank Account is a Debit account, any monies lodged to the bank are recorded on the debit side of the journal.

2. The second entry is the record of the money retained in petty cash. This entry will be posted to the Petty Cash Account in the Nominal Ledger. Since the Petty Cash Account is a bank account, then this entry will be on the debit side of the journal.

3. The third entry in the record of the capital which was invested in the company. This entry will be posted to the Capital Account in the Nominal Ledger. Since the Capital account is a credit account (which will be explained later) then this entry is entered on the Credit side of the journal.

Once you enter the nominal account number for the Bank Current A/C and the Petty Cash account the program will display the following warning:

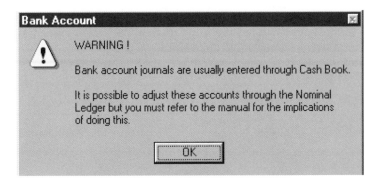

This warning appears because, as explained above, this entry would normally be entered through the Cash Book in the computerised bookkeeping system. However, if you are using this method to enter the Capital Investment, when the entries have been completed the screen should look like the following:

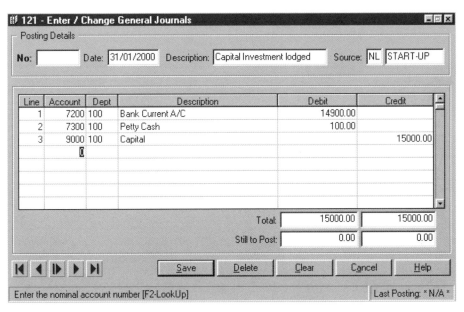

[S] **Save** and the following window will appear:

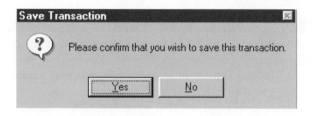

[S] **Yes** and the posting is complete.

13. Nominal Ledger

The Nominal (General) Ledger consists of a number of accounts which are used to record the Income, Expenditure, Assets, Liabilities and Owner Equity in the company. Every transaction which occurs in the company must eventually be recorded in the nominal ledger. Figures are transferred from sales ledger, purchase ledgers and cash book automatically. The figures in the nominal accounts are used in producing a Trial Balance which we will be doing later.

Nominal accounts will be one of five possible types Income, Expense, Asset, Liability or Owner Equity, as described on page 41 for manual bookkeeping. Each type of account will be either a Debit (Dr) or Credit (Cr) account. This means that if an account is a Credit account then the balance in that account will normally be a Credit amount. If an account is a Debit account then the balance in that account will normally be a Debit amount. The computer will automatically assign an account as 'Debit A/C' or 'Credit A/C' depending on the type entered.

Enter/Create Nominal Accounts

The nominal accounts which will be required by the company must be created in the Nominal Ledger before they may be used when entering data. You have already been using a number of nominal accounts as at least two must be used in order to make a valid entry in the accounts.

Task C-24

Enter (Create) the following Nominal Accounts:

Number	Description	Type	Dr or Cr
3000	Salaries	Expense	Dr
3200	Electricity	Expense	Dr

New Nominal accounts are created as follows:

[S] 1 Nominal
[S] 1 Nominal Accounts
[S] 1 Maintain Chart of Accounts

The program will then present the 'Maintain Chart of Accounts' screen.

The creation of a new account only requires the input the following information for each nominal account:

NL Account Details

Number: Enter the account number for this account.

Group: Accounts may be grouped for reporting purposes.
               (Enter the new group name to set-up a new group or press the F2
               function key for a list of groups). Press the Tab key to accept
               DEFAULT.

Description: Enter a description for this account.

Type: Select from list. (Asset, Expense, Income, Liability, Owners Equity)

Dr or Cr: Select Debit A/c if this account normally has a Debit balance.

               Select Credit A/c if this account normally has a Credit balance.

               Press the Tab key after Type, and the program will display the
               correct entry for this field.

After inputting the above data the screen will look like the following:

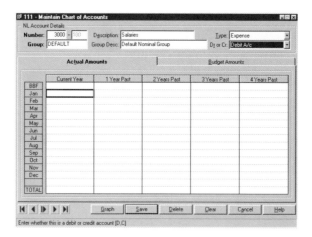

[S] Save to save this account.

Repeat the procedure for the Electricity Account.

Nominal Ledger Account Enquiry

All transactions entered in the company books must appear in one of the nominal accounts. Any nominal account may be examined at any time by simply displaying that particular account. Since this report does not affect the files it may be examined as often as you like.

Task C-25

Display the Current Bank A/C from the Nominal Ledger.

A nominal account is displayed as follows:

[S] 1 Nominal

[S] 1 Nominal Accounts

[S] 2 Nominal Ledger Account Enquiry

The program will then present the 'Nominal Ledger Account Enquiry' screen. The selections to be made from this screen are as follows:

Account

Account Number: Enter the nominal account number.

Department: 100 will automatically be displayed

Date Range

Year: The Current year will be displayed but you may select past years for which details are required.

Starting Period: Period 1 will be displayed but you may enter any starting period.

                    Note: The first period is the first month of the financial year, not necessarily January.

Ending Period: Period 1 will be displayed as we are still dealing with month 1. The program will normally automatically display the period number which you are currently working in.

                    The Starting and Ending Dates will automatically be displayed when the periods are entered.

Include

Include Opening Balance: Tick this box to display the opening balance for this account

---

When the data has been entered the screen will look like the following:

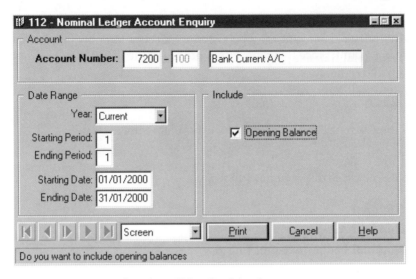

[S] **Print** and the account details will be displayed on screen.

When the report is displayed on the screen you may send it to the printer by simply clicking the Print button at the bottom of the report. Click the Cancel button if you do not want to send it to the printer. This will close the window and return you to the previous window, where you may look at another nominal account or click the Cancel button to close the window.

Print Trial Balance

As all entries in the accounts are automatically posted to the nominal ledger it is possible to produce a trial balance at any time. The computer simply prints the balances from each nominal account. Since all entries in the system were balanced as they were entered the trial balance will always balance. This does not mean that all the entries in the system were correct and the trial balance should be examined closely to make sure that it is correct.

Task C-26

Display a Trial Balance as at 31/01/##.

The term 'as at' is used in accounting to mean from the start of the financial year up to the date stated.

A trial balance is produced as follows:

[S] 1 Nominal
[S] 3 Reporting
[S] 4 Print Trial Balance

The program will then present the Print Trial Balance screen. The selections to be made from this screen are as follows:

Date Range

Year: The Current year will be displayed but you may select past years for which a trial balance is required.

Starting Period: Period 1 and the date will be displayed but you may enter any starting period.

Note: The first period is the first month of the financial year, not necessarily January.

Ending Period: Period 1 and the date will be displayed as we are still dealing with month 1. The program will normally automatically display the period number which you are currently working in.

Include

Include: The boxes for 'Opening Balances' and the 'Year-to-date Figures' should be ticked.

When the data has been entered the screen will look like the following:

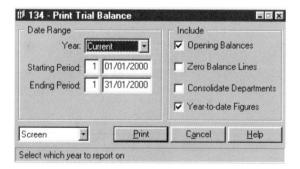

[S] Print and the Trial Balance will be displayed on screen. The report may be sent to the printer in the normal way.

NOTE: *Compare this Trial Balance with the one produced manually for the same period. Both Trial Balances should be exactly the same*

14. Customers and Suppliers

A company will normally have a number of customers and suppliers. All information about customers including transactions is stored in the Sales Ledger. All information about suppliers including transactions is stored in the Purchase Ledger.

Set Up New Customer and Supplier

In order to enter Invoices, Credit Notes, Receipts, Payments, etc. the standing data, such as Name, Address, Phone No., etc. must be set up for each customer and/or supplier.

Task C-27

Set up the standing data for the customer and supplier listed below:

Customer			Supplier	
Code	D001		**Code**	P102
Name	Francis Dunne		**Name**	Power Ireland
Address	Cutlery Road		**Address**	Park West
	Newbridge			Navan
	Co Kildare			Co Meath
Phone	045-433258		**Phone**	046-253672
Fax			**Fax**	046-253489
e-mail			**e-mail**	info@powerirl.ie

The procedure for setting up customers and suppliers is practically identical, so the following steps relate to both customers and suppliers. Standing data is set-up as follows:

Customers	*Suppliers*
[S] 2 Sales	**[S] 3 Purchase**
[S] 1 Customers	**[S] 1 Suppliers**
[S] 1 Maintain Customers	**[S] 1 Maintain Suppliers**

The program will then present a screen for the input of the standing data for each customer/supplier.

This screen contains four different sections, General, Miscellaneous, Delivery Address and NL Distribution. These are displayed as tabs under the customer/supplier code and name and may be selected by simply clicking on the tab name. You may ignore a lot of the data on the various sections.

The data which you will need to input, is contained on the general section and is as follows:

Customer/ Supplier Code:	The code for this customer/supplier.
Name:	The name of this customer/supplier.
Also a Customer /Supplier:	If this customer/supplier is also a supplier/ customer, then change the No to Yes. Accept 'No' by pressing the Tab key.
Address:	The customer's/supplier's address.
Telephone:	Customer's/supplier's telephone number.
Fax:	Customer's/supplier's fax number.
Email:	Customer's/supplier's e-mail address
Note:	*Use the Tab key to move from field to field and to skip a field.*

When you have entered the above information the screen should look like the following for entering a customer.

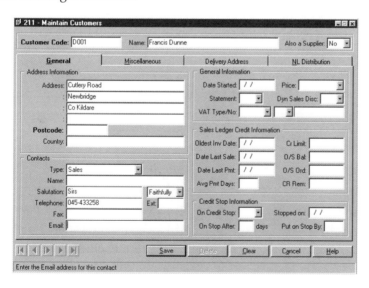

[S] Save to save this customer/supplier.

The program will then display the following window:

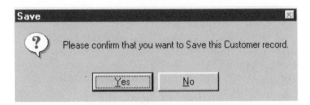

[S] **Yes** and the customer/supplier is saved.

You may then input another customer/supplier or [S] **Cancel** which will close that window and return to a blank screen.

Unallocate/Delete Receipt or Payment

Sometimes a receipt or payment may have been allocated incorrectly or the payment may have been entered to the wrong customer's or supplier's account. If the receipt/payment has been allocated incorrectly, then it must be unallocated. If it was entered to the wrong account then it must be deleted in order to be entered and allocated to the correct account. During the un-allocation procedure you may decide whether just to un-allocate and retain the receipt/payment or to delete it altogether.

Task C-28	**(Optional)**

Unallocate and delete the receipt from James Mahon.

Receipts or Payments are Unallocated as follows:

Customers	*Suppliers*
[S] **2 Sales**	[S] **3 Purchase**
[S] **5 Receipts**	[S] **5 Payments**
[S] **2 Unallocate/Delete Sales**	[S] **2 Unallocate/Delete Purchase**
Ledger Receipts	**Ledger Payments**

The program will then display a screen for the input of some data.

The data to be input is as follows:

Customer/Supplier Details

Code and Name: Enter the customer's/supplier's code and press the Tab key. The Name will be displayed automatically.

(If you press the F2 function key the program will display a list of customers/suppliers)

Start Date: Enter a date to start the search for receipts or payments. In cases where there are large volumes of receipts/payments, entering a start date is a simple method of reducing the amount of receipts/payments which will be displayed.

Display: You must click Display the Display button in order to display the receipts/payments. Alternatively you may press the enter key when the display button is active (highlighted).

Note: *Use the Tab key to move from field to field and to skip a field.*

Enter the data and **[S] Display**.

When you click on Display the screen will look like the following:

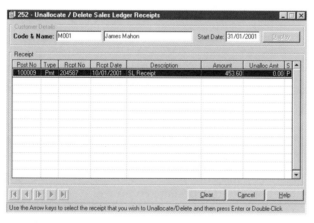

Select the receipt/payment to be unallocated by using the arrow keys or the mouse (if there is more than one), and press the enter key.

 NOTE: *If you point to the receipt/payment and double click the mouse button the receipt/payment will be deleted and you will not have the option of just unallocating it.*

Once the receipt/payment is highlighted and you press the enter key and the following screen will be displayed:

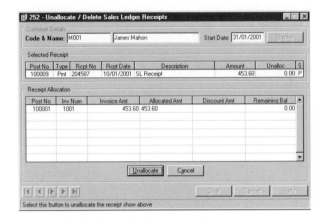

[S] Unallocate and the following window will appear:

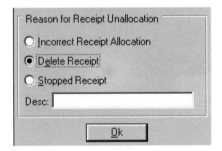

At this stage you may decide whether to just unallocate or to delete the receipt/payment altogether.

[S] Delete Receipt   (By pointing to Delete Receipt and click the left mouse button. The black dot should now appear in circle in front of Delete Receipt.)

[S] OK and the unallocation and deletion are complete.

Task C-29   (Optional - but must be performed if Task C-28 is completed.)

Enter and allocate the receipt on Source Documents page 8 from James Mahon.

This will restore the company files to the position they were in before we deleted the receipt.

15. Products and Services

In order to produce an invoice using the invoicing section of a computerised book-keeping program it is necessary to have the details about the products and services, which the company is selling, entered in the computer records. Each product is given a code which is then used to access that product for the purpose of issuing invoices and credit notes.

Enter Product Details

The computer program offers a special section for entering the details about products and services.

Task C-30

Add the following product in the list of products:

Code	Description	VAT Rate	Retail Price
T122	22′ Solon TV	1 – 20%	€299.00

The task of adding products to the list of products and services is as follows:

[S] 5 Products

[S] 1 Products / Services

[S] 1 Maintain Products / Services

The program then presents a screen for the input of the required data for each product/service.

The top of this screen is headed Product Code and Description and requires the input of the following:

Product Code and Description

Code: Enter the code for this Product/Service.

Description: Enter the description for this Product/Service here.

The rest of the screen has two sections, with tabs labelled **Product Details** and **Assembly**. The Assembly section is for the input of the parts which make up an assembly (we will not be dealing with such items). The Product Details section requires the input of the data for each product. The program will prompt you, at the bottom of the screen, with what is required to be entered in each field.

The data to be entered is detailed below. Press the Tab key to skip the fields where you do not have to enter data. In some cases the program will enter default values and in other cases the field will remain blank.

Product Details

Type and Pricing

Product Type: Select from one of three types: **Assembly**

Non stock item [i.e. Service]

Regular stock item.

In our case we will be dealing with regular stock items so press the Tab key to accept this option.

VAT Rate: Select the appropriate VAT rate for this Product/Service.

(Press the F2 key to display the list of VAT codes).

Press the Tab key to accept the default values for Goods/Service, Group, Description, Bar Code, Last Sale, and Cost Price.

Note: Do not enter the Price in the Cost Price field.

Sell Price 1: Enter the full retail price for this item.

Press the Tab key to skip Sell Price 2 and 3.

Nominal Ledger Distribution

Sales Account: Enter the Nominal Sales Account Code (1000) or the Repairs Account Code (1100). Press the Tab key to accept the code offered if it is the correct one.

(Press the F2 key to display the list of Nominal account codes.)

Cost Account: Press the Tab key to accept the code offered.

Stock Account: Press the Tab key to accept the code offered.

When you have entered these details the screen should look like the following:

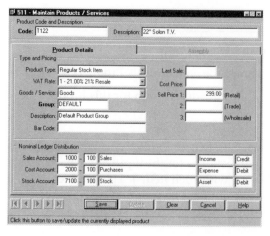

[S] Save and the following window will appear:

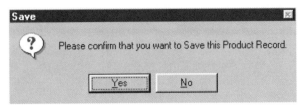

[S] **Yes** and the product will be saved.

Task C-31

Add the following products in the list of products:

Code	Description	VAT Rate	Retail Price
C101	Compact Disc Player (Philem)	1 – 20%	€85.00
V102	Panview VCR	1 – 20%	€249.00

Print Product Details

The product details report is used to print the details for products/services as input above.

Task C-32

Print the Details of all products for J.P. Murphy Electric

This option to print the products/services details is selected as follows:

[S] 5 Products
[S] 3 Products / Services Reporting
[S] 1 Print Product Details

The program then displays a screen allowing the input of some options as shown below:

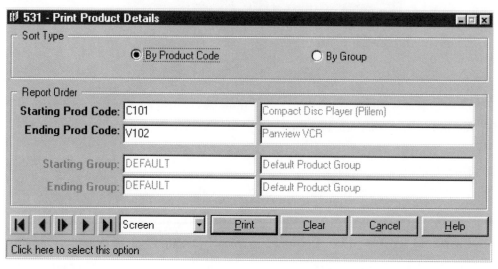

The options which are displayed are correct so simply **[S]** **Print** to display the report.

When a report is displayed on screen you may produce a hard copy by simply **[S]** **Print** at the bottom of the screen report.

16. Report Printing

There are a great number of reports which may be obtained from the various ledgers. Running these reports causes the program to search the company files and assemble the required information in an understandable format. The running of any of these reports does not update the files and they can therefore be run as often as required.

The presentation of the reports is defined by the program and it is therefore only necessary to select the report required and input some simple selections for each report. Each report will provide prompts with the most likely options and generally it is only necessary to press the Tab key to accept the options offered. The prompt line at the bottom of the screen will provide instructions with what to input each time a piece of data is required.

Most reports require the input of the Starting and Ending Periods or the Starting and Ending Dates for the report. When inputting Starting and Ending periods (months) it must be remembered that period 1 is the first period of the financial year for the company. This can be any month of the year, and not necessarily January. The period numbers are then counted from the first month of the financial year.

When a report is displayed on screen you may produce a hard copy on the printer by simply **[S] Print** at the bottom of the report. Click the Cancel button if you do not want to send it to the printer. This will close the window and return you to the previous window, where you may look at another report or **[S] Cancel** to close the window.

The following Reports have already been explained. The numbers in brackets indicate the menus which are selected to produce the report. The page number is the page number in this book where the report is explained.

Sales Order Enquiry	(6 1 2)	Page 83
Sales and Cash Daybooks	(2 4 1)	Page 91
Customer Account Enquiry	(2 1 2)	Page 92
Purchase and Cash Daybooks	(3 4 1)	Page 102
Supplier Account Enquiry	(3 1 2)	Page 103
Nominal Ledger Account Enquiry	(1 1 2)	Page 117
Print Trial Balance	(1 3 4)	Page 118
Print Product Details	(5 3 1)	Page 127

VAT Report

The VAT report provides the details which are required for filling in the VAT 3 form.

> ### Task C-33
>
> Produce a VAT 100 report for January ##.

The VAT 100 report is produced as follows:

[S] 0 Central

[S] 3 VAT Rates / Reporting

[S] 3 Print / Submit VAT 100 Form

When this option is selected the program displays a screen for the input of some selections, as shown below:

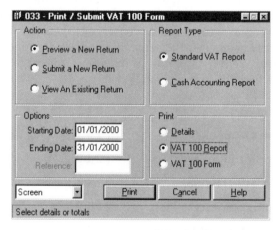

[S] VAT 100 Report from the Print options and the **[S] Print**.

The report will be displayed on screen and gives the information necessary to complete the VAT 3 form.

Aged Debtors' Report

This is one of the most common reports to be produced on a computerised bookkeeping system. The report shows all the customers who owe money to the company.

Task C-34

Produce an Aged Debtors report as at 31 January ##.

The Aged Debtors' report is produced as follows:

[S] 2 Sales Ledger
[S] 4 Sales Ledger Reports
[S] 2 Print Aged Debtors Report

When this option is selected the program displays a screen for the input of some selections, as shown below:

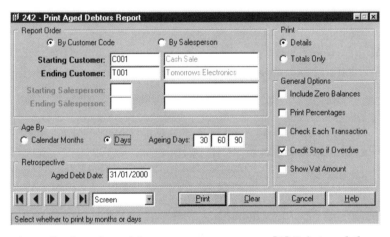

The options displayed on this screen are correct so **[S] Print** and the report will be displayed on screen showing details of all customers who owe money to the company.

Aged Creditors' Report

This shows all the suppliers who the company owe money to.

Task C-34

Produce an Aged Debtors report as at 31 January ##.

The Aged Creditors' report is produced as follows:

[S] 3 Purchase Ledger
[S] 4 Purchase Ledger Reports
[S] 2 Print Aged Creditors Report

When this option is selected the program displays a screen for the input of some selections, as shown below:

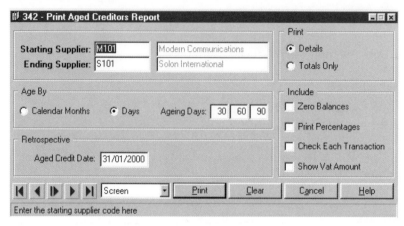

The options displayed on this screen are correct so **[S] Print** and the report will be displayed on screen showing details of all suppliers who are owed money by the company.

Cash Book Payments and Receipts Reports

These are reports which are displayed very often as it shows a listing of all monies paid out and received by the company. These reports should not be confused with the receipts and payments reports from the sales and purchases ledger. These reports must be produced for each bank account separately, so it is necessary to produce separate reports for the Bank Current A/C and Petty Cash.

> **Task C-36**
>
> Produce a Cash/Cheque Payments and Receipts report for January ##.

Since the Task asks for a Cash/Cheque Payments and Receipts report, this automatically indicates that it is the Bank Current A/C which must be reported on.

The Cash/Cheque Payments and Receipts report is produced as follows:

[S] 4 Cash Book
[S] 4 Reporting
[S] 1 Print Cash Book Payments / Receipts

When this option is selected the program displays a screen for the input of some selections, as shown below:

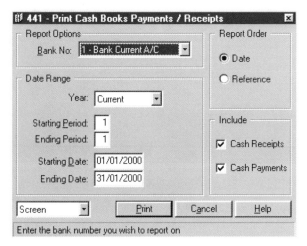

In this case the options offered are correct, with the options to print Cash Receipts and Cash Payments ticked, so **[S] Print** and the reports will be displayed on screen If you only needed one report then it is a simple matter of removing the tick from the report which is not required.

The reports are displayed with one report in front of the other. The second report may be displayed by pointing to the grey band beside the report name and clicking the left mouse button.

Petty Cash Payments Report

This report shows all the petty cash payments. Each item purchased from petty cash is listed on the report.

Task C-37

Produce a Petty Cash Payments report for January ##.

The Petty Cash Payments report is produced using the same options as for the Cash/Cheques Payments and Receipts report, as follows:

[S] 4 Cash Book

[S] 4 Reporting

[S] 1 Print Cash Book Payments / Receipts

When this option is selected the program displays a screen for the input of some selections. In this case you must select '2 – Petty Cash' as the Bank No:, and remove the tick from Cash Receipts as we only require the Petty Cash Payments report.

When these selections are made the screen should appear as shown below:

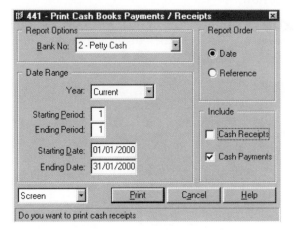

[S] **Print** and the report will be displayed on screen showing details of all petty cash payments for the month of January ##.

  Any report which is displayed on screen may be sent to the printer by [S]
NOTE: *Print on the screen report.*

17. Ledger Dates

When you start TAS Books Accounting Plus and enter the accounts for a particular company there will be four dates displayed at the bottom of the screen, as shown below:

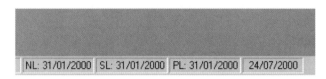

The four dates are the posting dates for the three ledgers and the present date. Some companies have all four dates set to the present date and therefore the dates will change automatically each day, as the program takes the data from the computer clock when it starts up.

However in some cases, such as an accountants office, work is done on a monthly basis and therefore the ledger dates, i.e. Nominal Ledger (NL), Sales Ledger (SL) and Purchase Ledger (PL) are set to the end of the month. In our case, since we will not be working with an actual company, the dates we will be using will not be present dates. We will use the end of month dates and therefore we will have to set the ledger dates at the start of each month, before entering any transactions for that month.

Setting the Ledger Date

The ledger date may be set at any time, but is normally performed at the start of each month.

> **Task C-38**
>
> Set the Nominal Ledger date to the last day of February ##

The ledger date is set as follows:

[S] 2 Sales
[S] 9 End of Period Programs
[S] 9 Change Sales Ledge Date

or

[S] NL: 31/01/2000 (at bottom of screen)
Double Click the left mouse button.

The program will display the Change Nominal Ledger Date window.

This window presents two options:

1. Enter the date required, i.e. the last day of the month.
2. Set to todays date at start up.

Type the new Date (Remember to type the digits only, you must not type the slashes.)

[S] Save to save new date.

Task C-39

Set the Sales Ledger and Purchase Ledger dates to the last day of February ##

18. Backup and Restore Company Data Files

It is frequently necessary to copy the data files to a floppy disk for backup storage and copy them from the floppy disk to the working folder when they are required again. In order to perform these operations, the company must be closed down.

The TAS Books program provides an option for these purposes. These options are available on the TAS Books Accounting Plus – Multi-Company Selection window. This window automatically appears when the program is started or it may be selected from the Taskbar, as described earlier by simply selecting it on the taskbar and clicking the left mouse button.

NOTE: *The company must not be open when backing up the data files.*

Task C-40

Backup the data files for J.P. Murphy Electric to a floppy disk.

Backup Company Data Files

1. Open the TAS Books Accounting Plus – Multi-Company Selection window. The window will appear as shown:

2. **[S] the Company**   (J.P. Murphy Electric will already be selected if that is the only company setup on the computer.)

3. **[S] Backup**   (by pointing to the Backup button and clicking the left mouse button)

The program will then display the following window:

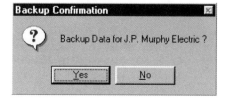

4.   **[S] Yes** and the following window will be displayed:

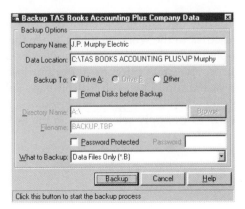

   There are two changes which should be made to the options displayed, which will assist in the Backup and Restore process. These changes are:

(a)   Remove the tick from the 'Password Protected' box

(b)   Select 'Data Files Only [*.B]' from the 'What to Backup' field as it is usually only necessary to backup the data files

5.   **[S] Backup** and the following window will be displayed:

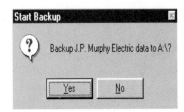

6.   **[S] Yes** and the following window, asking you to insert the first disk of a multi volume set, will be displayed:

7.   Insert a disk and **[S] OK**   (The backup of the data files will usually fit on a single disk but if not the program will prompt you to insert a second disk.)

The backup will start and the following progress window will be displayed:

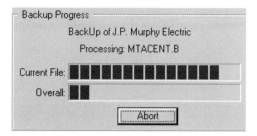

When backup is complete the following window will be displayed:

9.   **[S] OK** and the TAS Books Accounting Plus - Multi-Company Selection window will be displayed.

Task C-41

Restore the data files for J.P. Murphy Electric from the floppy disk.

Restore Company Data Files

1.   Open the TAS Books Accounting Plus – Multi-Company Selection window. The window will appear as shown:

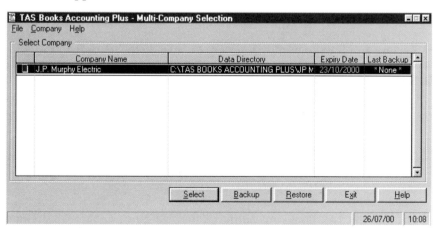

2.   **[S] the Company**   (J.P. Murphy Electric will already be selected if that is the only company setup on the computer.)

3.   **[S] Restore**   (By pointing to the Restore button and clicking the left mouse button.)

The program will then display the following window:

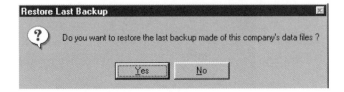

4.   **[S] Yes** and the following window will be displayed:

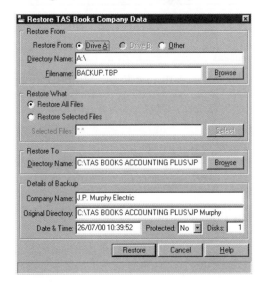

The data displayed is correct

5.   **[S] Restore** and the program will restore the files to the hard disk, and will briefly display a progress window as it does so. When complete the following window will be displayed:

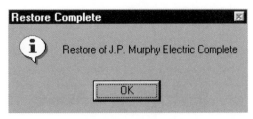

6.   **[S] OK** and the TAS Books Accounting Plus – Multi-Company Selection window will be displayed.

19. Transaction Summary

Source Documents

Sales Invoice

    (a) Create Sales Order in Invoice Section   Page 79
           6 Invoicing
               1 Sales Orders
                   1 Enter / Change Invoices / Cr Notes

    (b) Print and Post Sales Invoice   Page 81
           6 Invoicing
               2 Print / Post
                   5 Print Sales Invoices / Credit Notes

Sales Credit Note

    (a) Create Sales Order in Invoicing   Page 79
           6 Invoicing
               1 Sales Orders
                   1 Enter / Change Invoices / Cr Notes

    (b) Print and Post Sales Credit Note in Invoicing   Page 81
           6 Invoicing
               2 Print / Post
                   5 Print Sales Invoices / Credit Notes

    (c) Allocate Credit Note in Sales Ledger   Page 86
           2 Sales
               5 Receipts
                   1 Enter / Allocate Sales Ledger Receipts

Debtor Receipt

    Enter Receipt in Sales Ledger   Page 89
           2 Sales
               5 Receipts
                   1 Enter / Allocate Sales Ledger Receipts

Purchase Invoice

    Enter Invoice in Purchase Ledger   Page 94
           3 Purchase
               2 Enter / Change Journals
                   1 Enter / Change Supplier Invoices /
                     Credit Journals

Purchase Credit Note

    (a) Enter Credit Note in Purchase Ledger   Page 97
        3 Purchase
            2 Enter / Change Journals
                2 Enter / Change Supplier Credit Note /
                   Debit Journals

    (b) Allocate Credit Note in Purchase Ledger   Page 97
        3 Purchase
            5 Payments on Account
                1 Enter / Allocate Purchase Ledger
                   Payments

Creditor Payment

(Remittance Advice)   Enter Payment in Purchase Ledger   Page 101
        3 Purchase
            5 Payments on Account
                1 Enter / Allocate Purchase Ledger
                   Payments

Petty Cash Purchase

    Enter Purchase in Cash Book   Page 107
        4 Cash Book
            2 Enter / Change Journals
                2 Enter / Change Cash Payments / Purchases
                 (Use '2 - Petty Cash' as Bank account)

Non-Purchase Payment

(Salaries, Rent etc.)   Enter Payment in Cash Book   Page 105
        4 Cash Book
            2 Enter / Change Journals
                2 Enter / Change Cash Payments / Purchases
                 (Use '1 - Current Bank A/C')

Restore Petty Cash Imprest

    Calculate the amount to be transferred and enter as Non-Purchase
    Payment in Cash Book   Page 108
        4 Cash Book
            2 Enter / Change Journals
                2 Enter / Change Cash Payments / Purchases
                 (Use '1 - Current Bank A/C')

Enter Product Details
    Enter new product in Products   Page 125
      5 Products
        1 Products / Services
          1 Maintain Product / Service

Central

    Maintain Company Information.   Page 76
      0 Central
        1 General Company Information
          1 Maintain Company Information

    VAT 100 Report.   Page 130
      0 Central
        3 VAT Rates / Reporting
          3 Print / Submit VAT 100 Form

Nominal Ledger

    Enter Nominal Account Codes   Page 115
      1 Nominal
        1 Nominal Accounts
          1 Maintain Chart of Accounts

    Nominal Ledger Account Enquiry   Page 117
      1 Nominal
        1 Nominal Accounts
          2 Nominal Ledger Account Enquiry

    Entries in General Journal   Page 111
      1 Nominal
        2 Enter / Change Journals
          1 Enter / Change General Journals

    Print Trial Balance   Page 118
      1 Nominal
        3 Reporting
          4 Print Trial Balance

Cash Book

Products

Invoicing

20. Exercises C-1 and C-2

Exercise C-1

1. Create additional Customer Accounts for the customers listed on Source Documents page 19.

2. Create additional Supplier Accounts for the suppliers listed on Source Documents page 19.

3. Create additional Nominal Accounts from the details listed on Source Documents page 19.

4. Enter additional Products from the details listed on Source Documents page 19.

5. Create Invoices and Credit Notes from the details listed on Source Documents pages 20–21.

   Note: (*Remember to allocate the credit notes, and enter and allocate the receipt of the cash for the cash sale.*)

6. Enter the source documents on Source Documents pages 34–55 into the appropriate accounts.

7. A direct debit of €1532.75 was made for Salaries on 28/02/##. Enter this transaction in the appropriate accounts.

8. Cheque number 200207 was cashed on 28/02/## to restore the petty cash imprest to €100.00. Determine the amount of this cheque and enter the transaction in the appropriate accounts.

9. Produce the following printouts (these may be displayed on screen only): (Compare your reports with the Daybooks, Ledgers and Trial Balance obtained from Exercise M1)

   ● All Invoices and Credit Notes

   ● Trial Balance as at the last day of February ##

   ● Sales Daybook for February ##

   ● Purchases Daybook for February ##

   ● Cheque Payment report for February ##

   ● Petty Cash Payments for February ##

   ● Cheque Receipts for February ##

   ● Product Details

   ● VAT 100 Report

10. Extract a trial balance as at the last day of February ##.

11. Complete a VAT 3 form for the months of January and February ##.

12. Backup your data files to a floppy disk.

Exercise C-2

The following company has been set up on your computer:

> Gem Jewellers
> Patricks Street
> Cork City
> Co Cork

Carry out each of the following tasks:

1. Create Customer Accounts as follows:

Code	H001
Name	Thomas Higgins
Address	Main Street
	Middleton
	Co Cork

Code	P001
Name	Power's Emporium
Address	James Street
	Cork
	Co Cork

Code	C001
Name	Cash Sale
Address	

Code	H002
Name	High Street Jewellers
Address	New Street
	Fermoy
	Co Cork

Code	F001
Name	Margaret Finn
Address	Wilton Villas
	Rochestown
	Cork

Code	C002
Name	The Crown Jewels
Address	Main Street
	Blarney
	Co Cork

2. Create Supplier Accounts as follows:

Code	G101
Name	The Gold Warehouse
Address	Western Park
	South Ring
	Cork

Code	E101
Name	Exclusive Jewellery
Address	Edwards Street
	Cork
	Co Cork

Code	M101
Name	Modern Communications
Address	City West Park
	Naas Road
	Co Dublin

3. Create the following additional Nominal accounts:

Number	Description	Type	Dr or Cr
● 1100	Repairs	I	Cr
● 3000	Salaries	E	Dr
● 3100	Rent	E	Dr
● 3200	Electricity	E	Dr
● 3300	Telephone	E	Dr
● 3400	Post	E	Dr
● 3500	Stationery	E	Dr
● 3600	Cleaning	E	Dr
● 3700	Miscellaneous Expenses	E	Dr
● 9000	Capital	O	Cr

4. Enter the following product details:

Product	Stock Code	VAT Rate	Selling Price
Sapphire Pendant	P111	20%	€185.00
Gold Necklace	N111	20%	€125.00
50cm Gold Chain	C111	20%	€95.00
Gold Bracelet	B111	20%	€85.00
Repairs	R100	12.5%	€18.50

5. The company commenced business on 01/01 ## with capital of €25000.00, depositing €24,800.00 in their current bank account and €200.00 in their Petty Cash account. Enter this information in the appropriate accounts.

6.   Create Sales Invoices and Credit Note from the details shown below. Print and Post each of these documents.

Invoices

Date	Customer	Product Code	Qty.
03/01/##	Thomas Higgins	N111	10
		B111	6
07/01/##	Powers Emporium	P111	2
		R100	8
09/01/##	Cash Sale	R100	7
		B111	5
11/01/##	Powers Emporium	C111	8
		B111	2
13/01/##	Cash Sale	R100	4
15/01/##	The Crown Jewels	P111	5
		C111	10
19/01/##	High Street Jewellers	N111	8
		P111	2

Credit Note

Date	Customer	Product Code	Qty.
19/01/##	Thomas Higgins	N111	3
		B111	2

7.   Enter the source documents on Source Documents pages 69–81, into the appropriate accounts.

8. Enter the following Direct Debit payments into the appropriate accounts:

    ● Rent Payment of €450.00 on 25/01/##

    ● Salary Payment of €1108.56 on 30/01/##

9. Cheque No. 215014 was cashed on 31/01/## to restore the Petty Cash imprest to €200.00. Determine the amount of this Cheque and enter the transaction into the appropriate accounts.

10. Produce the following printouts.

    ● All Invoices and Credit Notes

    ● Trial Balance as at 31 January ##

    ● Sales Daybook for January ##

    ● Purchase Daybook for January ##

    ● Cheque Payment report for January ##

    ● Petty Cash Payments for January ##

    ● Cheque Receipts for January ##

    ● A List of Product Details

    ● VAT 100 Report

11. Extract the following from the VAT 100 report:

    ● The amount of VAT which would be payable or repayable to (or from) the Collector General for January ##.

12. Backup your files to a floppy disk.

PART IV

INSTALLATION
AND
COMPANY SET UP

21. Installing TAS Books Accounting Plus

In order to perform the computerised tasks set out in this book it is necessary to have a computerised accounting/bookkeeping program on your computer. As already mentioned, this book may be used with any computerised accounting/bookkeeping program but the displays in the book are from TAS Books Accounting Plus. This section deals with the installation of that program on a computer or computer network.

Stand Alone Computer

The following notes details the installation of TAS Books Accounting Plus on a stand alone computer, running Windows 95/98/2000. It is advisable to shut down all programs before installing any new program. Any computer attached to a network can be treated as a stand alone computer.

1. Place the TAS Books Accounting Plus CD in the CD Disk Drive and close the drive.

2. If Autorun is set up on your computer then the CD will start automatically after a few seconds (allow 10 to 20 seconds before deciding autorun is not setup). If autorun starts proceed to step 3.

    If Autorun is not set up, proceed as follows:

    [S] Start on the Taskbar

    [S] Run from the pop up menu and the following window will be displayed:

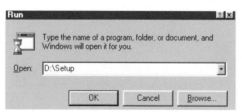

Type D:\Setup (In the Open field where D is the letter of your CD Disk Drive.)

[S] OK and the installation program will start

3.   When the installation program starts the following window will be displayed:

[S] Install TAS Books Accounting Plus for the first time and the following window will be briefly displayed:

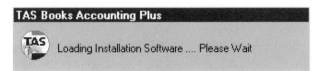

4.   The program will then display the Welcome window as shown below:

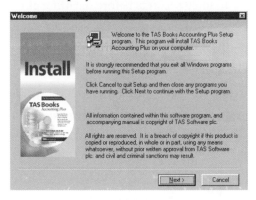

This window recommends that you close all other programs before proceeding.

[S] Next to continue with the setup.

5.   The program will then display the user identification screen, requesting the name of your company. The serial number of your program will be displayed automatically.

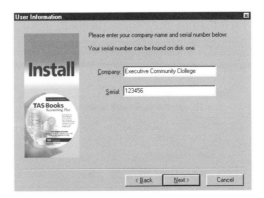

Type your School/College Name

Type Your Serial Number   (Your serial number is on the inside of the CD box.)

[S] Next

6.   The following Registration Confirmation window will be displayed:

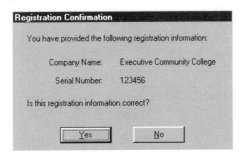

The information should be correct.

[S] Yes

7.   The choose installation option window will then be displayed.

[S] Single User (by pointing to the large square button under Single User with the single computer icon on it)

8.   The program will then display the choose destination folder window.

The information displayed here should be correct.

[S] Next

9.   The program will then display the select program folder window.

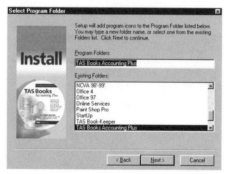

The program has chosen a folder, named TAS Books Accounting Plus.

[S] Next

10.   The installation process will then start and the following window will be displayed showing the percentage completed as it progresses.

When the installation is nearing completion the following window will also appear:

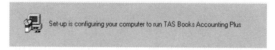

11. When the installation is complete the following window will be displayed allowing you to place a shortcut icon on your desktop. This shortcut allows you to start the program by simply double clicking on the shortcut icon. A window will appear similar to the following:

    [S] Yes

12. The setup complete window will then be displayed:

Remove the CD from the CD Drive

    [S] Finish   The computer will shut down and automatically restart.

22. Setting Up a New Company on Computer

The TAS Books Accounting Plus Program is a multi-company program. This means that you may create and work on more than one company's accounts. However, it is necessary to set up each company separately. When the program is installed there is no company set up so it is therefore necessary to set up at least one company in order to start using the program. The program is supplied with a demonstration company which you may install and work with if you wish. The following steps detail the procedure for setting up a new company

1.   Load the program in the normal way by double clicking on the TAS Books icon on the desktop. The program will display the TAS Books Accounting Plus – Multi-   Company Selection window as shown below:

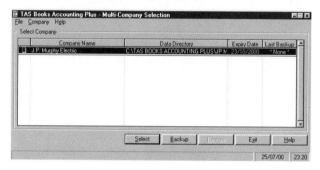

[S] Company menu   (point to the company menu and click the left mouse button)

[S] New Company (from the drop down menu)

NOTE: *The first time you load the program the following screen will be displayed. This screen displays a message in front of the Multi-Company Selection window telling you that you must create a new ompany. The procedure for doing this is exactly the same whether it is the first company or subsequent companies.*

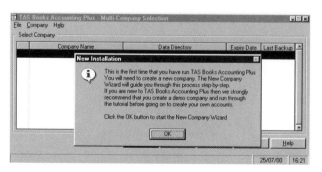

[S] OK

2. The program will then display the New Company Wizard. This will guide you through the setting up of a new company.

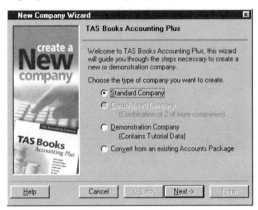

The program will automatically select Demonstration Company, which we do not want (unless you are specifically setting it up for learning purposed)

[S] Standard Company (by pointing to the words Standard Company or the circle in front of them and clicking the left mouse button)

[S] Next

3. The program will then display the window shown below, asking you to enter some information about the new company to be created.

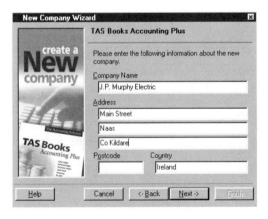

Enter the company Name and Address.

[S] Next

4. The program then displays the screen shown below. This screen offers a particular Company Status and Type of Business. We can accept these as we will be creating our own accounts later.

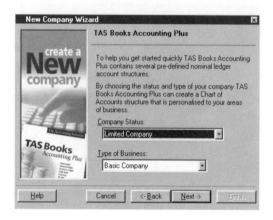

[S] Next

5. The program will then display the next screen for the selection of monthly accounting or 13 period accounting and the Book Year Start Date. Both these pieces of information are important, particularly the Book Year Start Date, as this is the start date for this company.

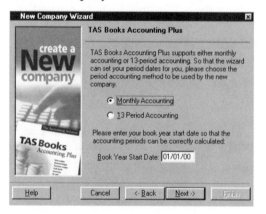

Accept the Monthly Accounting.

Enter the start date for this company.

6. The next window allows you to select the option of calculating VAT on a cash basis rather than an invoicing basis. We will not be using the Cash Accounting System.

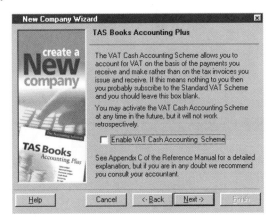

   [S] Next

7. The next window nominates the folder which will contain the company accounts. You must name the company folder only.

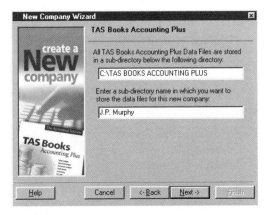

Type the name for the company Folder   (It is useful to use a name which
relates to the company.)

(Teachers may wish to use separate names for different class groups.)

8.   The next window displays all the information which you entered for this company. Check that the information is correct, and if it is not you may go back by selecting the Back button.

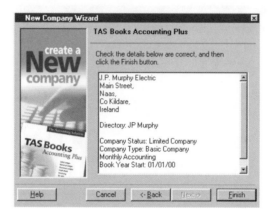

   [S] Finish   (A Progress Screen will be displayed showing the tasks being performed.)

9.   When installation is completed the Finish button will become active again as shown below.

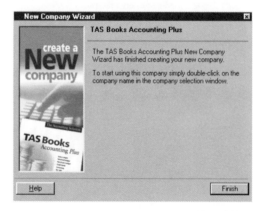

   [S] Finish

10. The program will then return you to the TAS Books Accounting Plus - Multi-Company Selection Window as shown below.

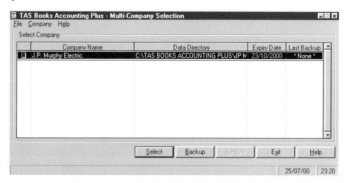

The new company will be listed in this window. A company is selected by high-lighting it and clicking on the Select button in this window. Alternatively a company may be selected by double clicking on the company name. Once selected the company Login Screen will be displayed as shown below:

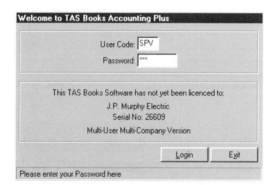

Type the User code –   **SPV**   (SPV stands for supervisor).

Type the Password –   **SPV**   (three asterisks will appear instead of the letters SPV).

NOTE: *It is advisable to change the password for the SPV user code as SPV is the standard password provided with all TAS Books programs.*

The company is now created but the correct Nominal Accounts, VAT rates, Customers, Suppliers and Products must still be set up for this company. The procedure for setting up a new company is detailed next.

23. Create Default Structure for a Company

Before it is possible to start inputting data into a company accounts there are a number of Nominal Accounts, VAT rates, Bank Accounts, Default accounts and structures which must be set up first. When the new company was created the program created Nominal Accounts, VAT account, Bank Accounts and Default accounts. However, it is much better to create these accounts yourself as the accounts and structures created by the program are not the most suitable for training purposes. We will therefore delete all the accounts and start from scratch.

The complete process is detailed in the following pages.

1. **Load the company**. This is accomplished in the normal way by double clicking on the TAS Books icon on the desktop to load the TAS Books Accounting Plus – Multi-Company Selection window. The program will display the TAS Books Accounting Plus – Multi-Company Selection window as shown below:

If you have just created the company then this window will already be open.

[S] Company   (Point to the company name and click the left mouse button then [S] Select. Alternatively the company may be selected by pointing to the company name and double click the left mouse button.)

2. **Login to the company**. When the company is selected the Login Screen will be displayed as shown below:

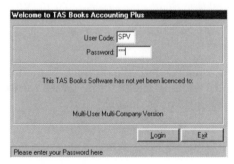

Enter **SPV** for User Code and press the TAB key.

Enter **SPV** for Password.

[S] Login

3. **Register the company**. In order to perform this task you will need the registration number received from TAS Software when you returned the registration form. If you did not return the registration form you will not have receivedyour registration number and you will not be able to perform this task.

    [S] 0 Central
    [S] 4 User Password Maintenance
    [S] 8 Product Registration

    The program will then display the product registration window as shown below:

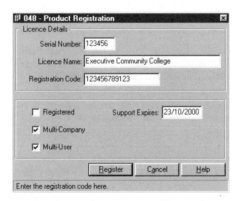

Enter the Licence Name **exactly** as received for TAS Software.

Enter the Registration Code **exactly** as received.

[S] Register

NOTE: *The company name must be typed exactly as on the registration letter, including any spaces, full stops, upper and lower case letters.*

4. **Cleardown the Data Files.** This task removes all the data from the company which the program has just created and will allow you to create the company exactly as you require. This task is accomplished as follows:

    [S] 0 Central
    [S] 4 User Password Maintenance
    [S] 9 Cleardown Data Files

The following screen will then be displayed:

[S] All Data   (by pointing to 'All Data' and clicking the left mouse button.)

[S] Cleardown

The program will then display the following warning message:

[S] Yes and the program will display the following progress window

When the process is complete the following window will be displayed:

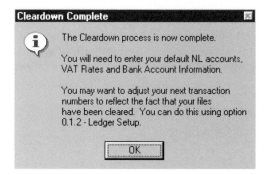

[S] OK and the cleardown is complete.

5.   **Setup new user.** This task creates another user with a separate password which may be used by other users of this company. These users may have full or limited rights with regard to updating the company files. A new user is setup as follows:

[S] 0 Central

[S] 4 User Password Maintenance

[S] 2 Maintain Passwords / User Access Rights

The screen will then be displayed for the input of the new user details.

Enter the New User in the 'User' field.

Enter a Name for the new user in the 'Name' field.

Enter a Password in the 'Password' field.

Enter the same Password in the 'Confirm Password' field.

Tick Supervisor Rights (this must be ticked if you wish to allow this user to edit the company name).

Tick the Edit Transactions Box.

Tick the Require Password Box.

The screen should then look like the following:

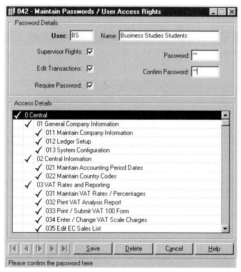

[S] **Save** and the new user will be saved.   (You may have to scroll down the screen to see the Save button.)

This is also the process used to change the Supervisors (SPV) password. In which case it is only necessary to enter the new password twice, once in the Password field and once in the Conform Password field and [S] **Save**.

[S] ☒ on the top right corner of the window, to close the window

6.   **Renumber Suspense Account.** When the data file cleardown took place the program left one nominal account. This account is 2500 Suspense Account. The first thing we will do is renumber this to 9999 Suspense Account as follows.

[S] 0 Central

[S] 5 General Operations / Utilities

[S] 3 Change Nominal Account Number

The Change Nominal Account screen will then be displayed with the following warning message:

[S] OK and the warning will disappear.

Enter the number 2500 in the Account Number field of the Current Account Details and press the Tab key. The account name will be displayed automatically

Enter the number 9999 in the Account Number field of the New Account Details

The screen should then look like the following:

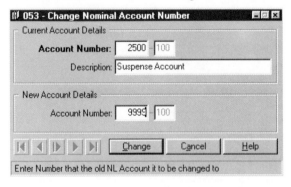

[S] Change   the following window will be displayed when the renumbering has been completed:

[S] OK

[S] ☒ on the top right corner of the window, to close the window

7. **Create the Nominal Accounts** which are listed in the table below. Some of these accounts are required as default accounts in order to set up the company. The other accounts are required in order to carry out the tasks set for J. P. Murphy in this book, and are generally some of the accounts which would be required by all companies.

The accounts shown in bold print are the default accounts and are the ones which must be set up when creating a new company. These accounts have special significance to the program and if they are not set up the program will display a warning message when logging into the company.

Account '9999 Suspense Account' will already be set up as this is the account which was renumbered in the previous step. This account is also a default account.

The details on how to set up Nominal accounts are contained on page 115.

Nominal Accounts

Number	Description	Type	Dr or Cr
1000	**Sales**	**Income**	**Cr**
1100	Repairs	Income	Cr
2000	**Purchases**	**Expense**	**Dr**
3100	Rent	Expense	Dr
3300	Telephone	Expense	Dr
3400	Post	Expense	Dr
3500	Stationery	Expense	Dr
3600	Cleaning	Expense	Dr
3700	Miscellaneous Expenses	Expense	Dr
3999	**Unused Default**	**Expense**	**Dr**
7000	**Debtors**	**Asset**	**Dr**
7100	**Stock**	**Asset**	**Dr**
7200	**Bank Current A/C**	**Asset**	**Dr**
7300	Petty Cash	Asset	Dr
8000	**Creditors**	**Liability**	**Cr**
8100	**VAT Payable**	**Liability**	**Cr**
8200	PAYE/PRSI Payable	Liability	Cr
9000	Capital	Owner Equity	Cr
9100	**Retained Profit**	**Owner Equity**	**Cr**
9999	**Suspense Account**	**Owner Equity**	**Cr**

8. **Print the List of Nominal Accounts.** This task is accomplished as follows:

[S] 1 Nominal

[S] 3 Reporting

[S] 1 Print Nominal Account / Description

The program will then display a screen for the input of the Starting and Ending Account numbers. The options offer are correct and the screen should look like the following:

[S] Print and the list will be displayed on screen. [S] Print on the screen output and the list will be sent to the printer. It is handy to have this list at hand while completing the company setup.

[S] ✕ on the top right corner of the window, to close the window.

9. **Setup VAT Rates**. This task is accomplished as follows:

    [S] 0 Central

    [S] 3 VAT Rates / Reporting

    [S] 1 Maintain VAT Rates / Percentages

When you select this option the following warning will appear:

This System Maintenance Program warning appears each time you select a maintenance option.

[S] OK to continue.

The Maintain VAT Rates / Percentages is one of the options available from the Maintain Company Information but the VAT Rates should be set up here after Cleardown.

A Screen for the input of the VAT rates will be displayed. Input the following VAT Rates and Percentages:

Code	Rate	Acct	Dept	NL Description	Short Description
1	20%	8100	100	VAT Payable	20% Resale
2	12.5%	8100	100	VAT Payable	12.5% Resale
3	0%	8100	100	VAT Payable	0% Resale
4	0%	8100	100	VAT Payable	Exempt Resale
5	20%	8100	100	VAT Payable	20% Non-Resale
6	12.5%	8100	100	VAT Payable	12.5% Non-Resale
7	0%	8100	100	VAT Payable	0% Non-Resale
8	0%	8100	100	VAT Payable	Exempt Non-Resale
9	0%	8100	100	VAT Payable	Outside Scope Rate

In each case simply type the **Rate**, **Acct** and the **Short Description**. The program will complete the rest for each rate as you enter it.

When the rates are entered there are three default rates which must be selected. These are:

Default Standard Rate

Default Zero Rate

Outside Scope Rate (This rate is used where there is no VAT on a transaction)

Select the appropriate rate in each case as follows:

[S] ▼ beside the field for the rate to be selected. The nine rates will be displayed in a drop down menu. Point to the rate required and click the left mouse button.

When the rates have been entered and the selections made, the screen should look like the following:

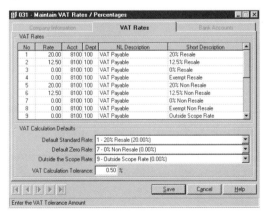

[S] Save and the VAT rates and percentages will be set up for this company.

10. **Setup Bank Accounts.** Bank accounts are set up as follows:

    [S] 4 Cash Book

    [S] 1 Bank Accounts

    [S] 1 Maintain Bank Accounts

    This System Maintenance Program warning appears again. **[S] OK** to continue.

    The Maintain Bank Accounts is one of the options available from the Maintain Company Information but the Bank Accounts should be set up here after Cleardown.

    Enter the following Bank Accounts

No	Acct	Dept	NL Description	Bank Account Name	Reconcile
1	7200	100	Bank Current A/C	Bank Current A/C	Y
2	7300	100	Petty Cash	Petty Cash	N

    Enter the Bank account nominal ledger number, the Bank Account Name and Y or N in the Reconcile column. (The current account will be reconciled and the petty cash will not be reconciled as there will be no bank statement for petty cash). The program will automatically fill in the other fields.

    When the bank accounts have been entered the screen will look like the following:

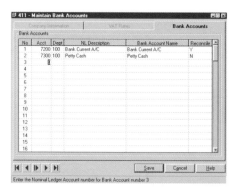

    [S] Save and the Bank Accounts will be set up for this company.

11. **Enter Company Information.** The basic information for this company was entered during the creation of the company. However we must now check this information and add the VAT Registration number for this company. This task is accomplished as follows:

    [S] 0 Central

    [S] 1 General Company Information

    [S] 1 Maintain Company Information

This System Maintenance Program warning appears again. **[S] OK** to continue.

The information displayed should be mostly correct with the exception of the Company VAT Number. Enter the county (IE) or select from the list and Enter the number (7584682P for J.P. Murphy Electric). The screen should then look like the following:

[S] Save and the General Company Information will be completed.

Do not setup VAT Rates and Bank Accounts from this option (011) after cleardown as it may cause an error and the process will have to be started again.

12. **Enter Data in Setup Ledgers.** There are a number of accounts and options which must be set up in the various ledgers. These are set up as follows:

[S] 0 Central

[S] 1 General Company Information

[S] 2 Ledger Setup

This System Maintenance Program warning appears again. **[S] OK** to continue.

The program then presents the Ledger Setup screen, with the Central Information section displayed. This screen has six sections for the input of the program default information. The six sections are labelled with tabs at the top of the screen. The six sections are:

0. Central Information,

1. Nominal Ledger,

2. Sales Ledger,

3. Purchase Ledger,

4. Cash Book,

5. Sales Orders.

There are a number of these default options which we will not be using so we will enter the Nominal Account '3999 Unused Defaults' as the Nominal account in such cases.

Enter the following data into the Central Information section:

0. Central Information

Next Transaction Numbers

Next Posting Number:	Accept 100001 as the next posting number
Dispatch Note Number:	Enter 1001
Sales Order Number:	Enter 1001
Sales Invoice Number:	Enter 1001

System Wide VAT Options

Always enter VAT Distribution:	Select No
Calculate VAT:	Select Before Settlement Discount

Ageing Periods

Accept options offered.

[S] Nominal Ledger by pointing to the tab labelled Nominal Ledger and clicking the left mouse button. The Nominal Ledger section will then be displayed.

When you select the Nominal Ledger section the following Window will be displayed. This window will appear each time you select a section, other than the Central.

[S] OK and continue.

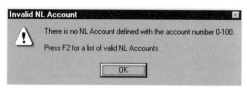

Enter the following data into the Nominal Ledger section.

1. Nominal Ledger

Default Nominal Ledger Accounts

Nominal Suspense Account:	Enter 9999
Retained Earnings Account:	Enter 9100
Write Off Account:	Enter 3999

Nominal Ledger Options

Accept the options displayed

[S] Sales Ledger

Enter the following data into the Sales Ledger section.

2. Sales Ledger

Default Sales Ledger Accounts

Sales Ledger (Debtor):	Enter 7000
Sales Account:	Enter 1000
Discounts Given:	Enter 3999

Sales Ledger Options
Accept COA mode

Sales Ledger Payment Adjustment Options

Bank Charges:	Enter 3999
Under-payments (Write-Off):	Enter 3999
Over-payments (Write-Back):	Enter 3999
Currency Gain/Loss:	Enter 3999
Other Gain/Loss:	Enter 3999

[S] Purchase Ledger

Enter the following data into the Purchase Ledger section.

3. Purchase Ledger

Purchase Ledger Accounts

Purchase Ledger (Creditors):	Enter 8000
Discounts Received:	Enter 3999

Purchase Ledger Options
Accept the options offered for this section

Purchase Ledger Payment Adjustment Options

Bank Charges:	Enter 3999
Under-payments(Write-Back):	Enter 3999
Over-payments (Write-Off):	Enter 3999
Currency Gain/Loss:	Enter 3999
Other Gain/Loss:	Enter 3999

[S] Cash Book

Enter the following data into the Cash Book section.

4. Cash Book

Cash Book Options
  Accept COA for this section

[S] Sales Orders

Enter the following data into the Sales Orders section

5. Sales Orders

Stock Accounts
Cost of Sales:	Enter 2000
Stock:	Enter 7100
Stock Adjustment:	Enter 7100 (We may use this number as we will not be dealing with stock adjustments)

Sales Order Module Options
Accept the options in this part

When completed the Window should look like the following

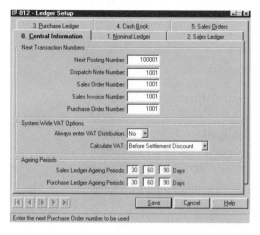

[S] **Save** and all six sections of information will be saved.

24. Create Additional Accounts and Products to start J.P. Murphy Electric

1. Set the Nominal, Sales and Purchase Ledger Dates to 31/01/2000 as described on page 135.

2. Set up Customer Standing Data from the customer details shown below. The procedure for maintaining customer standing data is detailed on page 120.

Code	M001
Name	James Mahon
Address	Willow View
	Prosperous
	Co Kildare

Code	E001
Name	The Electrical Shop
Address	The Mill
	Celbridge
	Co Kildare

Code	N001
Name	New Age Contractors
Address	Main Street
	Kilcullen
	Co Kildare

Code	C001
Name	Cash Sale
Address	

Code	T001
Name	Tomorrows Electronics
Address	Main Street
	Naas
	Co Kildare

3. Set up Suppliers' Standing Data from the supplier details shown below. The procedure for maintaining supplier standing data is detailed on page 120.

Code	S101
Name	Solon International
Address	Unit 12 Sunshine Ind Est
	Crumlin Rd
	Dublin 12

Code	P101
Name	Philem Ireland
Address	Unit 126
	Kenilworth Place
	Dublin 8

Code	M101
Name	Modern Comms
Address	City West Park
	Naas Road
	Co Dublin

4.　Enter Products from the product details shown below. The procedure for maintaining product details is detailed on page 125.

Code	Description	VAT Rate	Retail Price
T114	14' Solon T.V.	1 – 21%	€189.00
T116	16' Solon T.V.	1 – 20%	€229.00
V101	Philem VCR	1 – 20%	€245.00
R100	Repairs	2 – 12.5%	€14.80

NOTE:　*Ensure that the item 'R100 – Repairs' is entered as VAT rate '2 – 12.5% Resale' and as Sales Account 1100 instead of 1000.*

25. Installing a Company on Multiple Machines

The process of setting up the same company on a number of machines can be simplified by following the procedure detailed below:

1. Install the program on all machines. Ensure that you install the program in the same way on all machines. Use the same folder for the program in each case. Follow the procedure on pages 155–9.

2. Create the company on each machine. Follow the procedure for creating the company as detailed on pages 160–65 for each machine. Ensure that you use the same name and folder for the new company on each machine.

3. Setup the company on ONE machine only. Follow the procedure on pages 166–80.

4. Backup the Data Files only from the company which has been setup. The procedure for performing this task is detailed on page 137.

5. Restore the Backup files to each machine as detailed below:

    (i) Load the TAS Books Accounting Plus Program. The TAS Books Accounting Plus – Multi-Company Selection window will be displayed.

    (ii) Highlight the Company which has been created.

    (iii) Insert the disk with the Backup files in the floppy disk drive.

    (iv) **[S] Restore** the Restore window will appear. This window will allow you to restore the files from one company to a different company, but you must select the following options. Another window will appear in front of the restore window, asking if you wish to restore the last backup of this company's data files, as shown below.

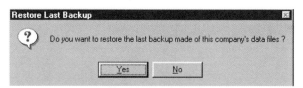

        [S] No as you have not backed up this company's files.

The message will disappear and the Restore window will be displayed. Enter the following options in this window:

Restore From –   **[S] Drive A:**

Filename –   **[S]** Browse the browse button beside the Filename field

The following window will then be displayed.

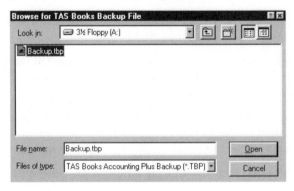

[S] **3½ Floppy [A:]** from Look in field

[S] **Backup file** (usually Backup.tbp)

[S] **Open**

The window will close and the Restore window will be displayed.

[S] Browse beside the Directory Name in the 'Restore to' section.

The following window will then be displayed.

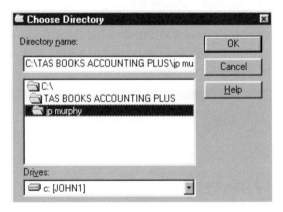

Select the Folder into which you wish to restore the Data Files.

> (The correct folder may already be selected or you may have to double click the left mouse button on the 'TAS Books Accounting Plus' folder to display the required folder, and then select the folder required.)

[S] **OK**

The window will close and the Restore window will be displayed.

The Restore window should now look like the following:

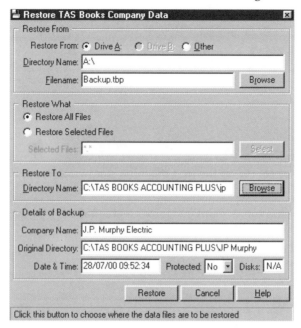

[S] Restore **- Restore**

The following warning window will then be displayed.

This is acceptable as you are not restoring the files belonging to the company created on this machine.

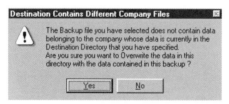

[S] Yes

The following progress screen will then be displayed briefly:

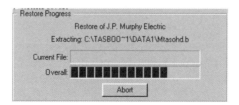

When the files have been restored the following window will be displayed:

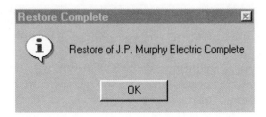

[S] OK

The company, as set up on the first machine is now active on this machine. You may select the company in the normal way.

Repeat the process for as many machines as required.

26. Setting up a Company - Summary

The following is a summary of all the steps detailed elsewhere in this book. Eventually you will only need this page to set up a new company.

The column labelled Menu is the three digit number which is used to select that particular option in TAS Books Accounting Plus. This option may be selected by holding down the Alt key and pressing each digit using the numbers on the top row of the keyboard.

The column labelled Page Ref is the page number in this book where the full detail of each operation may be found.

Step	Menu	Operation	Page Ref
1		Install TAS Books Accounting Plus	155
2		Create New Company	160
3		Load the Company	166
4		Login as Supervisor	166
5	048	Register the Company	167
6	049	Cleardown Data Files	167
7	042	Setup New User (Optional)	169
8	053	Renumber Suspense Account	170
9	111	Create Nominal Accounts	171
10	131	Print Nominal Accounts (Optional)	171
11	031	Setup VAT Rates	172
12	411	Setup Bank Accounts	174
13	011	Enter Company Information	174
14	012	Setup Ledgers	176
15		Set NL, SL &PL Dates (Optional)	135
16	211	Setup Customer Standing Data (Optional)	120
17	311	Setup Supplier Standing Data (Optional)	120
18	511	Enter Products (Optional)	125
19		Backup Data Files	137
20		Restore to other machines if required	181

PART V

SAMPLE
MANUAL ASSIGNMENT
AND
COMPUTERISED
EXAMINATION

27. Sample Manual Assignment

Manual Assignment

On completion of the examination the candidate must return the examination paper, source documents, daybooks, ledgers and answer sheets

Candidate Name: ———————————— *Date:* ——————————

Company Profile

Business Name:
Computer Services

Address:
Unit 106 Renwood Park Galway

Telephone:
091-556827

Fax:
091-556876

VAT Reg. No.:
IE4568942F

- Computer services are engaged in the sale and maintenance of computers. They purchase computers from a single source and peripherals from a different source.

- The company is registered for VAT

- The company is engaged in both cash and credit sales.

Instructions to Candidates

Carry out each task in the order in which they are listed.

1. The company commenced business on 1 January 2001 with capital of €60000.00, depositing €59800.00 in their current bank account and €200.00 in their Petty Cash account. Enter this information in the appropriate daybooks.

2. From the source documents provided, write up the following Books of Prime Entry:

    - Sales/Sales Returns Day Book
    - Purchases/Purchases Returns Day Book
    - Cash Receipts (Bank Lodgement) Book
    - Cash (Bank) Payments Book
    - Petty Cash Book
    - General Journal

3. Write up the following transactions in the appropriate Books of Prime Entry:

    - Rent Payment of €650.00 on 29 January 2001

4. Cheque No. 300103 was cashed on 31 January 2001 to restore the Petty Cash imprest (float) to €200.00. Determine the amount of this Cheque and enter the transaction into the appropriate daybook.

5. Post the entries in the Books of Prime Entry to the appropriate ledger accounts.

6. Balance all ledger accounts.

7. Extract a Trial Balance as at 31st January 2001.

8. Extract the required VAT details from the records and complete the VAT 3 form.

9.   Explain the following:

- creditor
- liability
- capital
- income
- computerised accounts.

28. Sample Solution and Marking Scheme – Manual Assignment Solutions

Sample Solutions

Sample Solutions

Company Name: Computer Services

Sales/Sales Returns Daybook

Month: January 2001

Date	Customer	F	Inv./Cr. Note Number	Total	Net Amount @ 20%	@ 12.5%	VAT Amount	←—Analysis —→ Sales	Repairs
04/01/01	James Kenny	SL	1001	€5250.00	€4375.00	—	€875.00	€4375.00	—
06/01/01	Mary Byrne	SL	1002	€1192.50	€825.00	€180.00	€187.50	€825.00	€180.00
08/01/01	Cash Sale	SL	1003	€1116.56	€825.00	€112.50	€179.06	€825.00	€112.50
10/01/01	Mary Byrne	SL	1004	€6540.00	€5450.00	—	€1090.00	€5450.00	—
12/01/01	James Kenny	SL	1005	(€2130.00)	(€1775.00)	—	(€355.00)	(€1775.00)	—
			Totals:	€11969.06	€9700.00	€292.50	€1976.56	€9700.00	€292.50
							NL	NL	NL

Cash Receipts (Bank Lodgement) Book

Month: January 2001

Date	Details	Lodge No.	F	Bank	Cash Sales	Debtors	Other
08/01/01	Cash Sale	100	SL	€1116.56	€1116.56	—	—
10/01/01	Mary Byrne (cheque 300248)	101	SL	€1192.50	—	€1192.50	—
11/01/01	James Kenny (cheque 400125)	102	SL	€3000.00	—	€3000.00	—
			Totals:	€5309.06	€1116.56	€4192.50	€0.00
				NL			

Purchases/Purchases Returns Daybook

Month: January 2001

Date	Supplier	F	Inv./Cr. Note Number	Total	Goods for Resale Net @ 21%	Net @ 12.5%	Goods N for R Net @ 21%	VAT Amnt.	←—Analysis —→ Purch.	Elec.	Tel.
03/01/01	Samala Inter.	PL	35781	€11700.00	€9750.00	—	—	€1950.00	€9750.00	—	—	—
04/01/01	Computer Periph.	PL	3487	€600.00	€500.00	—	—	€100.00	€500.00	—	—	—
13/01/01	Samala Inter.	PL	647	(€2340.00)	(€1950.00)	—	—	(€390.00)	(€1950.00)	—	—	—
14/01/01	Modern Communic.	PL		€99.24	—	—	€82.78	€16.54	—	—	€82.70	—
			Totals:	€10059.24	€8300.00	€0.00	€82.78	€1676.54	€8300.00	€0.00	€82.70	€0.00

Company Name: Computer Services

Cash (Bank) Payments Book **Month:** January 2001

Date	Details	Cheque No.	F	Total	Creditors	Salaries	Rent	Petty Cash	Other
							Analysis		
26/01/01	Modern Communications	300101	PL	€99.24	€99.24	—	—	—	—
29/01/##	Samala International	300102	PL	€9360.00	€9360.00	—	—	—	—
29/01/##	Rent Payment	DD	NL	€650.00	—	—	€650.00	—	—
31/01/##	Restore Petty Cash Imprest	300103	NL	€25.07	—	—	—	€25.07	—
	Totals:			€10134.31	€9459.24	€0.00	€650.00	€25.07	€0.00
				NL			NL	NL	

Petty Cash Book **Month:** January 2001

Date	Expenditure	Voucher No.	F	Total	VAT	Post	Stationery	Cleaning	Misc, Exp.
							Analysis		
05/01/##	Stamps	1	NL	€3.50	—	€3.50	—	—	—
05/01/##	Floppy Disks	2	NL	€6.24	€1.04	—	—	—	€5.20
15/01/##	Window Cleaning	3	NL	€10.13	€1.13	—	—	€9.00	—
18/01/##	Envelopes	4	NL	€5.20	—	—	€5.20	—	—
	Totals:			€25.07	€2.17	€3.50	€5.20	€9.00	€5.20
				NL	NL	NL	NL	NL	NL

General Journal **Month:** January 2001

Date	Details	F	Debit	Credit
01/01/##	Bank Current A/C	NL	€59800.00	—
01/01/##	Petty Cash	NL	€200.00	—
01/01/##	Capital	NL	—	€60000.00
	(Capital Investment Lodged)			
	Totals:		€60000.00	€60000.00

Company Name: Computer Services

Sales (Debtors) Ledger   **Customer:** James Kenny

Date	Details	F	Debit	Credit	Balance
04/01/01	Sales (Invoice 1001)	SB	€5250.00	–	€5250.00
11/01/01	Receipt (Cheque no. 400125)	CRB	–	€3000.00	€2250.00
12/01/01	Credit (Credit Note 1005)	SB	–	€2130.00	€120.00

Sales (Debtors) Ledger   **Customer:** Mary Byrne

Date	Details	F	Debit	Credit	Balance
06/01/01	Sales (Invoice 1002)	SB	€1192.50	–	€1192.50
10/01/01	Sales (Invoice 1004)	SB	€6540.00	–	€7732.50
10/01/01	Receipt (cheque no 300248)	CRB	–	€1192.50	€6540.00

Sales (Debtors) Ledger   **Customer:** Cash Sales

Date	Details	F	Debit	Credit	Balance
08/01/01	Sales (Invoice 1003)	SB	€1116.56	–	€1116.56
08/01/01	Receipt (Cash)	CRB	–	€1116.56	€0.00

Company Name: Computer Services

Purchases (Creditors) Ledger   **Creditor (Supplier):** Samala Intern.

Date	Details	F	Debit	Credit	Balance
03/01/01	Purchases (Invoice 35781)	PB	—	€11700.00	€11700.00
13/01/01	Returns (credit note no 647)	PB	€2340.00	—	€9360.00
26/01/01	Payment (cheque no 300102)	CPB	€9360.00	—	€0.00

Purchases (Creditors) Ledger   **Creditor (Supplier):** Computer Periph.

Date	Details	F	Debit	Credit	Balance
04/01/01	Purchases (Invoice 3487)	PB	—	€600.00	€600.00

Purchases (Creditors) Ledger   **Creditor (Supplier):** Modern Commun.

Date	Details	F	Debit	Credit	Balance
14/01/01	Telephone Bill (Invoice)	PB	—	€99.24	€99.24
26/01/01	Payment (cheque no 300101)	CPB	€99.24	—	€0.00

Company Name: Computer Services

Nominal (General) Ledger   **Nominal Account:** Sales

Date	Details	F	Debit	Credit	Balance
31/01/01	Sales (January 2001)	SB	—	€9700.00	€9700.00

Nominal (General) Ledger   **Nominal Account:** Repairs

Date	Details	F	Debit	Credit	Balance
31/01/01	Repairs (January 2001)	SB	—	€292.50	€292.50

Nominal (General) Ledger   **Nominal Account:** Purchases

Date	Details	F	Debit	Credit	Balance
31/01/01	Purchases (January 2001)	PB	€8300.00	—	€8300.00

Nominal (General) Ledger   **Nominal Account:** Rent

Date	Details	F	Debit	Credit	Balance
31/01/01	Telephone (January 2001)	CPB	€650.00	—	€650.00

Nominal (General) Ledger   **Nominal Account:** Telephone

Date	Details	F	Debit	Credit	Balance
31/01/01	Telephone (January 2001)	PB	€82.70	—	€82.70

Nominal (General) Ledger **Nominal Account:** Post

Date	Details	F	Debit	Credit	Balance
31/01/01	Post (January 2001)	PCB	€3.50	—	€3.50

Nominal (General) Ledger **Nominal Account:** Stationery

Date	Details	F	Debit	Credit	Balance
31/01/01	Stationery (2001)	PCB	€5.20	—	€5.20

Nominal (General) Ledger **Nominal Account:** Misc. Expenses

Date	Details	F	Debit	Credit	Balance
31/01/01	Misc. Exp. (January ##)	PCB	€5.20	—	€5.20

Nominal (General) Ledger **Nominal Account:** Cleaning

Date	Details	F	Debit	Credit	Balance
31/01/01	Cleaning (January 2001)	PCB	€9.00	—	€9.00

Nominal (General) Ledger **Nominal Account:** Bank Current A/C

Date	Details	F	Debit	Credit	Balance
01/01/01	Capital Investment	GJ	€59800.00	—	€59800.00
31/01/01	Bank Lodgements (Jan 2001)	CRB	€5309 .06	—	€65109.06
31/01/01	Cash Payments (Jan 2001)	CPB	—	€10134.31	€54974.75

Nominal (General) Ledger   **Nominal Account:** Petty Cash

Date	Details	F	Debit	Credit	Balance
01/01/01	Opening Balance	GJ	€200.00	—	€200.00
31/01/01	Total Payments (Jan 2001)	PCB	—	€25.07	€174.93
31/01/01	Restore Imprest	BPB	€25.07	—	€200.00

Nominal (General) Ledger   **Nominal Account:** VAT

Date	Details	F	Debit	Credit	Balance
31/01/01	VAT on Sales (January 2001)	SDB	—	€1976.56	€1976.56
31/01/01	VAT on Purchases (January 2001)	PDB	€1676.54	—	€300.02
31/01/01	VAT on Petty Cash Purchases (January 01)	PCB	€2.17	—	€297.85

Nominal (General) Ledger   **Nominal Account:** Capital

Date	Details	F	Debit	Credit	Balance
01/01/01	Capital Investment	GJ	—	€60000.00	€60000.00

Computer Services

Trial Balance as at 31/01/2001

	Debit	Credit
Sales		€9700.00
Repairs		€292.50
Purchases	€8,300.00	
Rent	€650.00	
Telephone	€82.70	
Post	€3.50	
Stationery	€5.20	
Cleaning	€9.00	
Miscellaneous Expenses	€5.20	
Debtors	€6660.00	
Bank Current Account	€54974.75	
Petty Cash	€200.00	
Creditors		€600.00
VAT Payable		€297.85
Capital		€60000.00
	€70890.35	€70890.35

In all correspondence please Quote

Registration No: IE **4568942F**

Notice No: 06334829-00040P

Office of the Revenue Commissioners
Collector-Generals Division
Sarsfield House
Francis Street
Limerick

Period: **01-01-2001**
31-01-2001

67839 151968 67521 1511481 000312VAT383

Computer Services
Unit 106
Renwood Park
Galway

Enquiries: 1800 203070

Payment due by:

VAT3 RETURN

Please print one figure only in each space using a black or blue ball point pen.

1. VAT

IRE : ENTER PUNTS ONLY

VAT ON SALES * T1 | | | | | 1 9 7 7 ·00

OFFICE USE ONLY
AMD A1 [ ]
O/S A2 [ ]

VAT ON PURCHASES ' T2 | | | | 1 6 7 9 ·00

Net Repayable | OR | Net Payable

T4 | | | | | | | ·00
(Excess of T2 over T1)

T3 | | | | | 2 9 8 ·00
(Excess of T1 over T2)

2. TRADING WITH OTHER EU COUNTRIES

Total goods to other EU countries

E1 | | | | | | | | ·00

Total goods from other EU countries

E2 | | | | | | | | ·00

3. BANK DETAILS FOR REPAYMENTS / REFUNDS

SORT CODE B1 | | | | | ACCOUNT NUMBER B2 | | | | | | |

*Only complete if you have not previously advised us of account details or you wish to amend previously submitted details.
Any repayment of VAT will be repaid to the bank or building society account as notified.*

I declare that this is a correct return of Value Added Tax for the period specified :-

Signed:- **<Student Name>**   Status:- **Student**   Date:- **31-01-2001**

🌀 **BANK GIRO**
CREDIT TRANSFER

Revenue 🏛️

To   BANK OF IRELAND
COLLEGE GREEN
DUBLIN 2

90-71-04

For   COLLECTOR-GENERAL
VALUE ADDED TAX
A/C NO. 31468191

Name: *Computer Services*
Period: **01-01-2001 – 31-01-2001**

Registration No. **IE 4568942F**
Notice No:

I declare that the amount shown below is the amount I am liable to remit to
the Collector-General for the above period.

Signed. **<Student Name>**   Date: **31-01-2001**

IR£

	IR£
CASH	
CHEQUES	298 - 00
TOTAL	298 - 00

VAT Payable	298	00

*Whole Punts
only. Please
do not enter
pence.*

*Receiving
Cashier's
Brand &
Initials*

Please do not fold this payslip or write or mark below this line.

VAT 3 IRE

⑈90⑈7104⑈ 31468191⑈ 80

Sample Marking Scheme

Manual Assignment

4 Sales Invoices   [Sales/Sales Returns Daybook]   *12 marks*
    Mark per invoice entered
        $^1/_2$ mark – date
        $^1/_2$ mark – detail
        $^1/_2$ mark – total inclusive
        $^1/_2$ mark – exclusive
        $^1/_2$ mark – VAT
        $^1/_2$ mark – analysis

3 Purchases Invoice   [Purchases/Purchases Returns Daybook]   *9 marks*
    Mark per invoice entered
        $^1/_2$ mark – date
        $^1/_2$ mark – detail
        $^1/_2$ mark – total inclusive
        $^1/_2$ mark – exclusive
        $^1/_2$ mark – VAT
        $^1/_2$ mark – analysis

2 Returns   [Sales/Sales Returns and Purchases/Purchases Returns
               Daybooks]   *6 marks*

    Mark per entry in Returns Book
        $^1/_2$ mark – date
        $^1/_2$ mark – detail
        $^1/_2$ mark – total inclusive
        $^1/_2$ mark – exclusive
        $^1/_2$ mark – VAT
        $^1/_2$ mark – analysis

2 Receipt   [Cash Receipts (Bank Lodgement) Book]   *4 marks*
    Mark per receipt
        $^1/_2$ mark – date
        $^1/_2$ mark – detail
        $^1/_2$ mark – bank
        $^1/_2$ mark – analysis

4 Payment   [Cash (Bank) Payments Book]   *8 marks*
    Mark per payment
        $^1/_2$ mark – date
        $^1/_2$ mark – detail
        $^1/_2$ mark – total
        $^1/_2$ mark – analysis

3 Petty Cash Payments   [Petty Cash Book]   *9 marks*
        Mark per item entered in Petty Cash Book
                $^1/_2$ mark – date
                $^1/_2$ mark – detail
                1 mark – amount
                1 mark – analysis

2 Debtors   [Sales (Debtors) Ledger]   *6 marks*
        Debtor James Kenny
                $^1/_2$ mark – sales amount
                $^1/_2$ mark – returns amount
                1 mark – bank amount
                1 mark – balance amount

        Debtor Mary Byrne
                $^1/_2$ mark – 1st sale
                $^1/_2$ mark – 2nd sale
                1 mark – bank
                1 mark – balance amount

3 Creditors   [Purchases (Creditors) Ledger]   *6 marks*
        Samala International
                $^1/_2$ mark – 1st purchase
                $^1/_2$ mark – bank
                $^1/_2$ mark – returns
                1 mark – balance amount

        Computer Peripherals
                $^1/_2$ mark – purchase
                1 mark – balance amount

        Modern Communications
                $^1/_2$ mark – purchase
                $^1/_2$ mark – bank
                1 mark – balance amount

10 Nominal Accounts   [Nominal (General) Ledger]   *24 marks*
      VAT a/c = 4 marks   [1 mark per transaction. 1 mark for balance]
      Bank a/c = 4 marks   [1 mark per transaction. 1 mark for balance]
      8 Other Accounts = 2 marks each

Trial Balance   [Trial Balance]   *4 marks*
        1 mark – list of accounts
        1 mark – debit figures
        1 mark – credit figures
        1 mark – total figures
                Deduct 2 marks for each item transferred incorrectly
                from ledgers to maximum of 4 marks
                Do not deduct for same error twice i.e. if account is
                incorrect in ledger, but is transferred to trial balance
                correctly, award mark.

VAT Form   [VAT 3 Form]   *3 marks*
        1 mark – T1
        1 mark – T2
        1 mark – T3

5 Bookkeeping terms   *5 marks*
        1 mark each for appropriate answer

Computerised
Examination

On completion of the examination the candidate must return the examination paper, source documents, daybooks, ledgers and print-outs

Candidate Name: _____ *Date:* _____

Company Profile

Business Name:

Computer Services

Address:

Unit 106 Renwood Park Galway

Telephone:

091-556827

Fax:

091-556876

VAT Reg Number:

IE4568942F

- Computer services are engaged in the sale and maintenance of computers. They purchase computers from a single source and peripherals from a different source.

- The company is registered for VAT.

- The company is engaged in both cash and credit sales.

- The required default accounts for the Sales Ledger, Purchase Ledger, Nominal Ledger and VAT codes have been created for the above company.

Instructions to Candidates

Carry out each task in the order in which they are listed.

1. **Create Customer Accounts as follows:**

Name	Code	Address
James Kenny	K001	Main Street Ballinasloe Co Galway
Mary Byrne	B001	Willowbank Salthill Co Galway
Cash Sales	C001	Cash Sales

2. **Create Supplier Accounts as follows:**

Name	Code	Address
Samala International	S101	Unit 12 Sunshine Industrial Est Crumlin Road Dublin 12 Tel: 01-868 2578
Computer Peripherals	C101	Unit 118 Kenwood Place Dublin 8 Tel: 01-646 4587
Modern Communications	M101	City West Park Naas Road Co Dublin Tel: 01-535 6274

3.   **Create Nominal Accounts as follows:**

Number	Description	Type	Dr or Cr
● 1100	Repairs	I	Cr
● 3100	Rent	E	Dr
● 3200	Electricity	E	Dr
● 3300	Telephone	E	Dr
● 3400	Post	E	Dr
● 3500	Stationery	E	Dr
● 3600	Cleaning	E	Dr
● 3700	Miscellaneous Expenses	E	Dr
● 9000	Capital	O	Dr

4.   **Enter the following product details:**

Product	Stock Code	VAT Rate	Selling Price
Computer	C111	20%	€ 825.00
Printer	P101	20%	€ 125.00
Repairs	R100	12.5%	€ 22.50

5.   The company commenced business on 1 January 2001 with capital of €60000.00, depositing €59800.00 in their current bank account and €200.00 in their Petty Cash account. Enter this information in the appropriate accounts.

6.   **Create** Sales Invoices and Credit Note(s) from the details shown below. **Print** and **Post** each of these documents.

Invoices

Date	Customer	Product Code	Qty
04/01/01	James Kenny	C111	5
		P101	2
06/01/01	Mary Byrne	C111	1
		R100	8
08/01/01	Cash Sale	R100	5
		C111	1
10/01/01	Mary Byrne	C111	6
		P101	4

Credit Note

Date	Customer	Product Code	Qty
12/01/01	James Kenny	C111	2
		P101	1

7.   **Enter** the source documents supplied on Source Documents pages 90–98, into the appropriate accounts.

8.   **Enter** the following Direct Debit payment into the appropriate accounts:

● Rent Payment of €650.00 on 29 January 2001

9.   Cheque No. 300103 was cashed on 31 January 2001 to restore the Petty Cash imprest (float) to €200.00. **Determine** the amount of this Cheque and **enter** the transaction into the appropriate accounts.

10.   **Produce** the following printouts. Printing may be performed after the examination time but no alterations may be made to the files.

- All Invoices and Credit Note
- Trial Balance as at 31 January 2001
- Sales Daybook for January 2001
- Purchase Daybook for January 2001
- Cheque Payment report for January 2001
- Petty Cash Payments for January 2001
- Cheque Receipts for January 2001
- Product Details
- VAT 100 Report

11.   **Extract** the following from the VAT 100 report:

- The amount of VAT which would be payable or repayable to (or from) the Collector General for January 2001. Enter this figure on the VAT 100 report form.

12.   **Backup** or **Copy** your data files to floppy disk.

30. Sample Solution and Marking Scheme

Computerised Examination

Computer Services	Invoice No:	1001
Unit 109	Invoice Date / Tax Point:	31/01/2001
Renwood Park	Page:	1
Galway		
Ireland		

VAT Number: IE-4568942F

Invoice to:

James Kenny
Main Street
Ballinasloe
Co Galway

Deliver to:

James Kenny
Main Street
Ballinasloe
Co Galway

| Your Ref: | **Desc:** Sales Invoice | **Customer Code:** K001 |
| Our Ref: 1001 | | **Order Date:** 04/01/2001 |

Description	V	Quantity	Price	Disc %	Total
Computer	1	5.00	825.00	0.00	4,125.00
Printer	1	2.00	125.00	0.00	250.00

VAT Rate	NET Amt	VAT Amt
1 20.00%	4,375.00	875.00

NET:	4,375.00
VAT:	875.00
TOTAL:	5,250.00

Produced by TAS Books Accounting Plus

Computer Services
Unit 109
Renwood Park
Galway
Ireland

Invoice No:	1002
Invoice Date / Tax Point:	31/01/2001
Page:	1

VAT Number: IE-4568942F

Invoice to:

Mary Byrne
Willowbank
Salthill
Co Galway

Deliver to:

Mary Byrne
Willowbank
Salthill
Co Galway

Your Ref:	**Desc:** Sales Invoice	**Customer Code:** B001
Our Ref: 1002		**Order Date:** 06/01/2001

Description	V	Quantity	Price	Disc %	Total
Computer	1	1.00	825.00	0.00	825.00
Repairs	2	8.00	22.50	0.00	180.00

VAT Rate	NET Amt	VAT Amt
1 20.00%	825.00	165.00
2 12.50%	180.00	22.50

NET:	1,005.00
VAT:	187.50
TOTAL:	1,192.50

Produced by TAS Books Accounting Plus

Computer Services	Invoice No:	1003
Unit 109	Invoice Date / Tax Point:	31/01/2001
Renwood Park	Page:	1
Galway		
Ireland		

VAT Number: IE-4568942F

Invoice to:

Cash Sale

Deliver to:

Cash Sale

Your Ref:	**Desc:** Sales Invoice	**Customer Code:** C001
Our Ref: 1003		**Order Date:** 08/01/2001

Description	V	Quantity	Price	Disc %	Total
Repairs	2	5.00	22.50	0.00	112.50
Computer	1	1.00	825.00	0.00	825.00

VAT Rate	NET Amt	VAT Amt
1 20.00%	825.00	165.00
2 12.50%	112.50	14.06

NET:	937.50
VAT:	179.06
TOTAL:	1,116.56

Produced by TAS Books Accounting Plus

Computer Services
Unit 109
Renwood Park
Galway
Ireland

Invoice No: 1004
Invoice Date / Tax Point: 31/01/2001
Page: 1

VAT Number: IE-4568942F

Invoice to:

Mary Byrne
Willowbank
Salthill
Co Galway

Deliver to:

Mary Byrne
Willowbank
Salthill
Co Galway

Your Ref:
Our Ref: 1004

Desc: Sales Invoice

Customer Code: B001
Order Date: 10/01/2001

Description	V	Quantity	Price	Disc %	Total
Computer	1	6.00	825.00	0.00	4,950.00
Printer	1	4.00	125.00	0.00	500.00

VAT Rate	NET Amt	VAT Amt
1 20.00%	5,450.00	1,090.00

NET:	5,450.00
VAT:	1,090.00
TOTAL:	6,540.00

Produced by TAS Books Accounting Plus

Computer Services
Unit 109
Renwood Park
Galway
Ireland

Credit Note No:	1005
Credit Note Date / Tax Point:	31/01/2001
Page:	1

VAT Number: IE-4568942F

Invoice to:

James Kenny
Main Street
Ballinasloe
Co Galway

Deliver to:

James Kenny
Main Street
Ballinasloe
Co Galway

Your Ref:	**Desc:** Credit Note	**Customer Code:** K001	
Our Ref: 1005		**Order Date:** 12/01/2001	

Description	V	Quantity	Price	Disc %	Total
Computer	1	2.00	825.00	0.00	1,650.00
Printer	1	1.00	125.00	0.00	125.00

VAT Rate	NET Amt	VAT Amt
1 20.00%	1,775.00	355.00

NET:	1,775.00
VAT:	355.00
TOTAL:	2,130.00

Produced by TAS Books Accounting Plus

Starting Period: BBF
Ending Period: 1

Computer Services
Trial Balance – Current Year (Inc BBF)

08/05/2001
3:32 pm

Acc	Dept	Description	Group	Period Debit	Period Credit	YTD Debit	YTD Credit
1000	100	Sales	DEFAULT		9,700.00		9,700.00
1100	100	Repairs	DEFAULT		292.50		292.50
2000	100	Purchases	DEFAULT	8,300.00		8,300.00	
3100	100	Rent	DEFAULT	650.00		650.00	
3300	100	Telephone	DEFAULT	82.70		82.70	
3400	100	Post	DEFAULT	3.50		3.50	
3500	100	Stationery	DEFAULT	5.20		5.20	
3700	100	Miscellaneous Expenses	DEFAULT	14.20		14.20	
7000	100	Debtors	DEFAULT	6,660.00		6,660.00	
7200	100	Bank Current A/C	DEFAULT	54,974.75		54,974.75	
7300	100	PettyCash	DEFAULT	200.00		200.00	
8000	100	Creditors	DEFAULT		600.00		600.00
8100	100	VAT Payable	DEFAULT		297.85		297.85
9000	100	Capital	DEFAULT		60,000.00		60,000.00
				70,890.35	70,890.35	70,890.35	70,890.35

Start: 01/01/2001
End :31/01/2001

Computer Services
(1) Sales Ledger– Sales Daybook

29/12/2000
4:09 pm

Post No	Post Date	Cust Code	Inv No	Inv Date	T	Description	Curr	Curr Amt	Net Amt	VAT Amnt	Tot Amnt
100003	31/01/2001	K001	1001	31/01/2001	1	Sales Invoice			4375.00	875.00	5250.00
100004	31/01/2001	B001	1002	31/01/2001	1	Sales Invoice			1005.00	187.50	1192.50
100005	31/01/2001	C001	1003	31/01/2001	1	Sales Invoice			937.50	179.06	1116.56
100006	31/01/2001	B001	1004	31/01/2001	1	Sales Invoice			5450.00	1090.00	6540.00
100007	31/01/2001	K001	1005	31/01/2001	N	Credit Note			−1775.00	−355.00	−2130.00

	Net Amt	VAT Amnt	Tot Amnt
Total Sales Invoices:	11,767.50	2,331.56	14,099.06
Total Credit Notes:	−1,775.00	−355.00	−2,130.00
Total Net Sales:	9,992.50	1,976.56	11,969.06
Total Debit Journals/ Refunds:	0.00	0.00	0.00
Total Credit Journals:	0.00	0.00	0.00
Total Journals:	0.00	0 00	0 00
Grand Total:	9,992.50	1,976.56	11,969.06

Start: 01/01/2001   **Computer Services**   29/12/2000
End :31/01/2001   (1) Purchase Ledger – Puchase Daybook   4:10 pm

Post No	Post Date	Supp Code	Inv No	Inv Date	T	Description	Curr	Curr Amt	Net Amt	VAT Amt	Tot Amt
100009 3	1/01/2001	S101	35781	03/01/2001	1	Purchase Invoice			9750.00	1950.00	11700.00
100010 3	1/01/2001	C101	3487	04/01/2001	1	Purchase Invoice			500.00	100.00	600.00
100011 3	1/01/2001	M101		14/01/2001	1	Purchase Invoice			82.78	16.56	99.34
100012 3	1/01/2001	S101	647	13/01/2001	N	Credit Note			−1950.00	−390.00	−2340.00

Daily Total for 31/01/2001	8,382.78	1,676.56	10,059.34
Total Purchase Invoices: 10,332.78	2,066.56	12,399.34
Total Credit Notes: −1,950.00	−390.00	−2,340.00
Total Net Purchase: 8,382.78	1,676.56	10,059.34
Total Debit Journals/Refunds: 0.00	0.00	0.00
Total CreditJournals: 0.00	0.00	0.00
Total Journals: 0.00	0 00	0 00
Grand Total: 8,382.78	1,676.56	10,059.34

Start: 01/01/2001				**Computer Services**					29/12/2000
End :31/01/2001				Payments Sorted by Date on Bank Current A/C					4:10 pm

Posting	Date	Code	Source	Payment Description	Ref	Rec	Curr	Curr Amount	Total
100019	31/01/2001	M101	PL 300101	PL Payment	300101	N			99.34
100020	31/01/2001	S101	PL 300102	PL Payment	300102	N			9360.00
100022	31/01/2001		CB300103	Transfer to PettyCash	300103	N			25.07
100023	31/01/2001		CB DD	Rent	DD	N			650.00
					Total Cash Payments:				10,134.41

Start Date: 01/01/2001
End Date: 31/01/2001

Computer Services
Payments Sorted by Date on Petty Cash A/C

29/12/2000
4:10 pm

Posting	Date	Code	Source	Payment Description	Ref	Rec	Curr	Curr Amount	Total
100013	05/01/2001		CB 000001	Stamps	000001	Y			3.50
100014	08/01/2001		CB 2	Floppy Disks	2	Y			6.24
100015	15/01/2001		CB3	WindowCleaning	3	Y			10.13
100016	18/01/2001		CB 4	Envelopes	4	Y			5.20

Total Cash Payments: 25.07

Start Date: 01/01/2001   **Computer Services**   02/04/2000

End Date: 31/01/2001   Cash Receipts Sorted by Date on Bank Current A/C   9:28 am

Posting	Date	Code	Source	Receipt Description	Ref	Rec	Curr	Curr Amount	Total
100001	01/01/2001		CB START	Startup Capital	START	N			59800.00
100012	31/01/2001	C001	SL Cash	Cash Sale	100	N			1116.56
100013	31/01/2001	B001	SL 300248	SL Receipt	101	N			1192.50
100014	31/01/2001	K001	SL 400125	ESL Receipt	102	N			3000.00

Total Cash Payments: 65,109.06

Start: C111
End: R100

Computer Service
Product Details

29/12/2000
4:10 pm

G/S	Code	Description	Typ	V	Group	Cost	Retail	Trade	Wholesale	Last Sale
G	C111	Computer	R	1	DEFAULT		825.00			12/01/2001
G	P101	Printer	R	1	DEFAULT		125.00			12/01/2001
G	R100	Repairs	R	2	DEFAULT		22.50			08/01/2001

Start Date: 01/01/2001
End Date :31/01/2001

Computer Services
VAT 100 Report

08/05/2001
3:33 pm

Description	Box	Amount
Computer Services		
VAT Reg No: GB–4568942F		
OutputTax	Box 1	1,976.56
Acquisition Tax on Goods from EC	Box 2	0.00
Total of Boxes 1 and 2	Box 3	1,976.56
Input Tax subject to normal rules	Box 4	1,678.71
Difference between Boxes 3 and 4	Box 5	297.85
Net Value of Sales	Box 6	9,992.50
Net Value of Purchases	Box 7	8,405.60
Net Value of Supplies of Goods to EC	Box 8	0.00
Net Value of Aquisition of Goods from EC	Box 9	0.00

Notes: This is a Preview only. Figures are subject to change.

VAT Due to Collector General for January = 297.85

Sample Marking Scheme

Computerised Examination

2 Customers   [Sales Invoice]   *6 marks*
    Marks per customer:
        1 mark – customer name
        1 mark – customer code
        1 mark – customer address

3 Suppliers   [Purchase Daybook]   *6 marks*
    Mark per supplier
        1 mark – suppliers name
        1 mark – suppliers code

3 Stock Items   [Product Details]   *6 marks*
    Mark per stock item
        1 mark – product and stock code
        $^1/_2$ mark – VAT code
        $^1/_2$ mark – selling price

8 Nominal Accounts   [Trial Balance]   *8 marks*
    Mark per each account
        $^1/_2$ mark – name
        $^1/_2$ mark – code

Capital Setup   [Trial Balance, Cheque Payments, Petty
                      Cash Payments]   *6 marks*
        3 x 2 marks

4 Sales Invoices   [Sales Invoices]   *12 marks*
    Marks per invoice
        $^1/_2$ mark – date
        $^1/_2$ mark – customer
        1 mark – product details
        1 mark – quantities

2 Receipts   [Cheque Receipts]   *6 marks*
    Mark per receipt
        1 mark – customer code
        1 mark – detail
        1 mark – correct account

3 Purchases invoices   [Purchase Daybook]   *9 marks*

    Mark per Invoice
           1 mark – correct account code
           1 mark – net amount
           1 mark – VAT

4 Payments   [Cheque Payments Book]   *12 marks*

    Marks per Payment
           1 mark – correct account
           1 mark – date
           1 mark – amount

2 Credit Notes   [Credit Note & Purchase Daybook]   *6 marks*

    Mark per Credit Note
           1 mark – customer or supplier code
           1 mark – items or amount
           1 mark – date

3 Petty Cash Payments   [Petty Cash Book]   *9 marks*

    Mark per item in petty cash account
           1 mark – date
           1 mark – total
           1 mark – correct account

Restore petty cash imprest   [Trial Balance]   *2 marks*

    Do not deduct for same error twice, i.e. if amount is calculated wrong in petty cash book but process is correct give marks.

Print 8 documents   *8 marks*
        1 mark for each appropriate document listed

Analysis/interpretation of one report

        2 marks

        0 mark – no understanding
        1 mark – some understanding
        2 mark – good understanding

Back-up data/copy data files   *2 marks*
        2 marks – if sufficient files copied to floppy disk.